Praise for
SHE WINS, YOU WIN

"The days of the 'fi[...] an anything are over. . . . Wome[...] to achieve power in the work v[...] ng one another at a disadvanta[...] out exactly how women should g[...]"
 —Kristen Kauffman, *The Dallas Morning News*

"A tremendous success in the rough and tumble world of television news, Evans knows the truths about women in business. Having long benefited from her insights, I am thrilled she has put them down on paper. Her game plan is a must read for working women."
 —Catherine Crier, Court TV anchor and author of
 The Case Against Lawyers

"This is the book men do NOT want women to read! Do you wonder why you are not running your corporation or business? Gail tells you how to change that! Gentlemen, move over."
 —Greta Van Susteren, host of Fox News Channel's
 On the Record with Greta Van Susteren

"*She Wins, You Win* supplies the missing piece of the puzzle to the troubling issue of why there are not more women in positions of power, particularly in business, and along with answering the 'why,' this book lays out the strategies for changing a losing dynamic into a 'win' for all women. I want every woman to read this book. It is perhaps the most important set of rules for women ever put forth."
 —Pat Mitchell, President and CEO, Public Broadcasting Service

GAIL EVANS is the author of *Play Like a Man, Win Like a Woman*, a phenomenal bestseller that has quickly become a classic in its field. A former White House Aide and CNN's first female executive vice president, Ms. Evans was responsible for creating some of CNN's most successful shows. She currently lectures around the country, mentoring and teaching women of all ages and business backgrounds how to get ahead in today's corporate world. She lives in Atlanta, Georgia, and has three children.

She Wins, *You* Win

The Most Important Strategies for Making Women More Powerful

Gail Evans

GOTHAM
BOOKS

GOTHAM BOOKS
Published by Penguin Group (USA) Inc.
375 Hudson Street, New York, New York 10014, U.S.A.
Penguin Books Ltd, Registered Offices: 80 Strand, London WC2R 0RL, England
Penguin Books Australia Ltd, 250 Camberwell Road,
Camberwell, Victoria 3124, Australia
Penguin Books Canada Ltd, 10 Alcorn Avenue, Toronto, Ontario, Canada M4V 3B2
Penguin Books (NZ) Ltd, Cnr Rosedale and Airborne Roads,
Albany, Auckland 1310, New Zealand

Published by Gotham Books, a division of Penguin Group (USA) Inc.
Previously published as a Gotham Books hardcover edition.

First Gotham Books trade paperback printing, May 2004

1   3   5   7   9   10   8   6   4   2

Gotham Books and the skyscraper logo are trademarks of Penguin Group (USA) Inc.

THE LIBRARY OF CONGRESS HAS CATALOGED THE
GOTHAM BOOKS HARDCOVER EDITION AS FOLLOWS:
Evans, Gail, 1941–
She wins, you win / by Gail Evans.
p.   cm.
ISBN 1-592-40025-6 (hc.)
1-592-40059-0 (pbk.)
1. Businesswomen.   2. Success in business.   I. Title.
HD6053 .E86 2003
650.1'082—dc21   2002043093

Printed in the United States of America
Set in Dante MT with OPTI Corvinus Light
Designed by Sabrina Bowers

This book is printed on acid-free paper. ∞

For Kathy and Jason, Laurie and Jeffrey, Greg and Julianna

Contents

Preface

Several years ago I gave a speech to a group of female lawyers. These women were bright and ambitious, but they felt stifled because they were not being made partners at the same rate as their male counterparts. The reason? According to their law firms, they were not bringing in enough business and, therefore, enough revenue.

As I listened to these women bemoan their situation, I realized that whenever I thought of hiring a lawyer, I instinctively called the husband of a friend or the man my father had used. I realized, too, that whenever I hired a stockbroker or an accountant, I also—unthinkingly—hired a man.

When I acknowledged this to the lawyers, they admitted that they tended to follow the same model—they also had hired male brokers and advisors. Most troubling was that even though these women knew that female accountants were having the same trouble making partner in their own firms, every one of these lawyers had a male accountant. (It wasn't all bleak, however: Two women had recently switched to female gynecologists.)

There we were, hardworking women with disposable income, handing out our business to the same people our fathers and brothers were using. This makes no sense. We're not getting ahead because we're not bringing in business, yet we continue to give away our own business to the men. Who is going to hire women if women don't?

As I was rising through the ranks of my own profession I hadn't thought of this kind of gender-related issue. I always believed that if you were smart, hardworking, politically adept, and reasonably easy to get along with, you would succeed—whether you were a woman or a man.

Most of my career seemed to support that notion. My first jobs were as executive assistants for congressmen in Washington, D.C. Though unquestionably the men had the more glamorous positions, my immediate bosses were women, and they were excellent. We all liked what we did, we were successful, and I had no reason to complain.

In 1966 I married a CBS news correspondent who was soon appointed bureau chief in Moscow. Once we moved there I became the de facto office manager, but because CBS had a nepotism rule, I couldn't be hired. Instead, I devoted myself to raising my three children. Then, after my husband was transferred back to America, I took on freelance jobs and began my own public relations and research company.

In 1980 CNN offered me a position and I went on to create the first central-booking department for any network. At this point in my life I assumed my goal was to keep up with the boys and that promotions would come based on the quality of my performance. I didn't feel any special connection to the other women employees, and I didn't fully understand what some of them were talking about when they came to me complaining about gender-related issues. I thought they simply weren't doing a good job playing the game.

My career flourished. In 1987, I was made a vice president at CNN; two years later I created *CNN & Co.*, the first television talk show to feature women discussing the major issues of the day, rather than what were considered "women's issues." After a promotion to senior vice president, I codeveloped *Talk Back Live*, the first interactive television news program, and in 1996 I was instrumental in creating *Burden of Proof*, the first daily legal talk show on network television. In 1996, I was made executive vice president of CNN.

Throughout this period I hired and promoted many women. But rather than consciously thinking about the need for women to help other women, I was preoccupied with other issues that successful women must cope with, such as impostor syndrome, from which I suffered. Despite all the wonderful jobs that kept coming my way, I feared I wasn't talented enough, and that someday my bosses would wake up and question my growing responsibility. After all, I had never been trained to do these tasks. I was always uncertain if someone else might not have done them better.

But slowly I grew more confident and was able to resolve most of my doubts. I also began to figure out the rules for the game of business—rules that had been written by men and that women had to know if they wanted to succeed. Eventually, that subject became the material of my first book—*Play Like a Man, Win Like a Woman*.

The more I thought about these rules, the more I realized that, like many women, I didn't want to play the game the way the guys did. I wanted to do it my way, remaining true to my value system, with my own individuality. As time passed I also began to realize that one of the most important elements of the men's game was missing from the women's. Whatever you want to call it—support, teamwork, assistance—the bottom line was: The boys were all taking care of each other. The women weren't.

Why would we object to helping another of our own gender? Why were we so reluctant to hire any women at all? We all watched, and felt left out, as the boss gave a job to his cousin or his fraternity buddy. But most of us were nervous about hiring too many women, because it seemed unfair, as though, once in power, we would now engage in our own brand of sexism.

The truth is, there's nothing wrong with what the men do. If the cousin ends up being incompetent, it won't do anyone any good. But what if the cousin is superb? What if your sorority sister is the best person for the job? Both of you will end up looking good.

In fact, why not do everything you can to help other women? Why are we still lending a hand to the men by not helping each other? It became obvious to me that although women face many obstacles in the business world, perhaps the most formidable is our interaction with other women.

Remember the famous quote from the old comic strip *Pogo*? "We have met the enemy and he is us." In too many instances, women are holding other women back by not putting them forward. We help each other in the small picture—

being supportive in times of trouble, giving advice about sticky job-related situations—but we are not helping in the big picture. We don't do enough rainmaking. We also don't create enough jobs. We don't provide adequate leadership. We don't go out of our way to help other women.

We must change all that because, like it or not, we're all in this together. And that's what this second book is about. It's time that we realize that whenever the woman down the hall, or in the building across the street, or in an office across the nation, wins a battle, we win a battle too. She wins, you win. It's that simple.

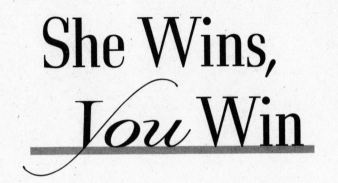

She Wins, You Win

PART 1

The Women's Team

1

Why You Must Play on the Women's Team

Let me tell you two very different stories. The first concerns Lily, a fiery young entrepreneur who started her own computer software business. This enterprise was so successful that a much larger firm eventually bought Lily out, but they asked her to continue running her company as an executive vice president. She accepted.

Unfortunately, Lily has run into a problem. The qualities that helped make her so successful as an entrepreneur—her independence and her verve—aren't necessarily working for her as a member of her new company's male-dominated corporate culture. It's clear to top management that while Lily's ideas are sharp and her company has proved to be an excellent acquisition, Lily herself isn't working out. The men aren't used to someone as openly passionate. Furthermore, Lily still acts as though she were running her own show, and without realizing it, she has been stepping on toes throughout the corporation.

As luck would have it, sitting on this company's board of directors is a well-known woman of great stature in this particular profession. She is fully aware that the board will do Lily in if she can't meld into the good old boy network. But this board member also sees how Lily's demeanor could be changed with some smart advice. So instead of taking the easy route of sitting back and watching Lily self-destruct, this woman, along with another top female executive, has decided to help—they are coaching Lily to get along better with the men, they are advising her on her management techniques, they are even modifying her choice of clothes, which are both too flashy and quirky, to blend in with the corporate culture.

To do so, these women are aware that they are risking political capital. The guys wouldn't be pleased to know that they're trying to save Lily's career—she's already history to them. But the women are well aware that as secure and nice as it is for them in such high positions, things will only change for women if they help the younger ones along.

So far, the word is that these women have made a difference, and that Lily has turned a corner. It looks as though she will make it after all.

The second story concerns Jenna, a fast-rising executive in the retail business. Jenna works at a company where most of the customers are women, and where half of the employees are women, but the firm itself is run entirely by men.

Recently these men have made it clear that they intend to add a woman to the senior vice president level. Jenna is certainly a candidate for this position, as are three other women.

But the pleasant camaraderie that existed between these women before the announcement was made is slowly disappearing. More than ever before the women see each other as rivals rather than compatriots, and the situation is becoming ugly. "We all know that there's room for only one of us," Jenna says. "And each one of us wants to be that one."

The women, divided and unhappy, are spending their time fighting among themselves, gossiping bitterly about each other, asking friends to support only one over the others, creating factions throughout the company. Meanwhile, the men above are watching warily. My fear is that none of the women will survive what is turning into an out-and-out war, or even if one does get the job, the others will have to leave.

My advice to Jenna: Try to find a way for the women to work together, because if they can't stop undermining one another, there may not be any female-friendly changes forthcoming at all.

The point is that it's only a win for women if *all* the women survive intact. If one of the women so bloodies the others that their reputations are badly damaged, it's not a win for the team. A real women's win is one where everyone fights fair and everyone is acknowledged for the effort, even if only one person ultimately is picked for the job.

• • •

I wish that stories like Lily's were more prevalent than stories like Jenna's. Unfortunately that's not the case, as I learned after the publication of my last book, *Play Like a Man, Win Like a Woman.* In that book I said that business is a game, and that men, having written all the rules, know how to play this game well. If women are to succeed, they need to know these rules so they can act out of knowledge rather than ignorance.

Due to the book's subject matter, I was invited to speak at seminars, conferences, and meetings around the world about the role of women in the workplace. The women in the audiences represented all levels of the business world, from top executives to entry-level assistants. And almost without exception, they found the book quite beneficial. They also realized that even if they didn't want to comply with some of the rules, they should at least know them all, and were setting about doing so.

But even though women are now playing the game of business more than ever, and better than ever, are we actually winning?

The answer is no. Statistics as well as my own observations bear this out. Time after time at these conferences I meet women, like Jenna, who have everything going for them: They're intelligent, they're ambitious, they're talented—but they aren't climbing the corporate ladder as fast and as far as they should.

I hear their frustration in the questions they ask me at the end of each speech, I hear it in the comments they make to each other, I see it in the e-mails and letters they send me.

"I'm smart, I work hard, I'm successful," they say, "but I feel that I'm playing the game alone." "I don't know whose team I'm on." "I have no place to go whenever something upsetting happens to me and I need advice."

Or they ask: "When one of my best friends was promoted over me, we stopped being friends—why does this happen?" "Why do women always become one of 'them' when they get promoted?" "Why does my female boss talk so much about helping other women, but, when the moment of truth arrives, she hires men?" "Why do so many women often act much tougher toward the women who work for them than the men do?"

They also ask: "Why is it that the women in my department are always there to support one another when someone fails, but when someone gets promoted, they distance themselves from her?"

A rising young comer at a major investment-banking company told me that one of her male coworkers took her to lunch and said that everyone in her group was upset because she was generating too much revenue (the others were all men). She left work that day bewildered and confused. Was she supposed to make less money for the company?

"You work at one of the most aggressive places in the world," I said, "and you took this man's complaint seriously? Do you honestly think your CEO feels that you're making too much money for him?"

Once she heard the idea uttered aloud, she realized how ridiculous the conversation had been. She even started to laugh. But because she had no one to talk to about it openly, the humor hadn't been evident before.

Another woman, an executive at a large public relations outfit, told me that all the men around her were vice presidents, yet she wasn't—even though she did as much work and had as much responsibility. When she finally got up enough nerve to ask her boss for a promotion, he said, "You're doing an excellent job, but we're not into titles at this company."

She left his office feeling she had violated some secret code and decided not to mention it again. Still, she couldn't help but wonder—if the company wasn't into titles, why did all the men seem to have them?

"Did you discuss this with the other women at your company?" I asked.

"No," she said. She felt the other women were her rivals so she didn't feel comfortable bringing up the subject. I suggested that one reason why none of the women had received the titles was because they kept the information to themselves, never discussing any of these issues with the others.

• • •

These questions and stories all have different scenarios and outcomes, but they represent something that I hadn't considered when I wrote my first book, which presents the rules of business as written by the men. The more I thought about it, the more I decided that women needed rules of their own, rules that apply only to women.

But when I sat down to write these rules, I came to realize that there's only one rule that will help eliminate women's confusion and unhappiness. There's only one rule that matters, one rule that I have not seen written about in any book, article, or Web site.

That one rule is: *Every woman must always play on the women's team.*

Why?

Because every time any woman succeeds in business, your chances of succeeding in business increase. And every time a woman fails in business, your chances of failure increase.

Women aren't playing on the same team with each other right now. We don't talk to each other. We don't support each other. We don't rainmake for each other. We act as though we were a minority at work (which is barely true) with no hope of ever changing that situation (which isn't true at all).

Like it or not, women are indeed treated like a minority in the world of business. But are we really? Women currently constitute a healthy (and growing) 47 percent of the work force. But we make up only 12 percent of the upper executive ranks. And female enrollment in business schools has plummeted over 15 percent in the past five years—in part because women are being given the message that while a business school education can help for the first ten or so years of a career, after that the playing field stops being level.

There's more. Women comprise only 12.5 percent of corporate officers, and only 12.4 percent of the board seats, in five hundred of America's largest companies. We represent only 4 percent of the top earners, and only 6.2 percent of the clout titles (chairman, chief executive officer, chief operating officer, vice chairman, president, senior executive vice president, and executive vice president). There are just four women CEOs in the entire Fortune 500.

Comparatively, we don't make enough money, either. Women who worked full-time, year-round in 2000 earned only 73 percent of what men who also worked full-time, year-round earned, according to the U.S. Census Bureau. The wage gap has narrowed by about ten percentage points during the last seventeen years, with only slight improvements in the most recent years.

A recently released Congressional study shows that the difference in managerial salaries for men and women actually increased from 1995 to 2000, despite the fact that the country was experiencing an economic boom. In certain key industries where women are supposedly making great strides (entertainment, communications, finance, insurance, and retailing), the gap increased by as much as twenty-one cents for every dollar.

There is a widely held perception that in the not-for-profit world women do much better than men, but the reverse is true. A new study from GuideStar, a national database on not-for-profit organizations, shows that over three quarters of the larger organizations are run by men. Alarmingly, even when women hold top positions, they earn, on average, significantly less money than their male counterparts—$170,180 compared to the men's $264,602.

Some of this lack of financial parity occurs because, as I said, women don't band together in ways that create power.

But it's also because women have been reluctant to admit that by banding together, we are more likely to succeed.

As a result, we are constantly being forced to second-guess ourselves, even when we decide to follow all the male rules. We are always expected to jump through hoops without understanding why. That's because our own way isn't the accepted way. The female's psyche is not the role model for the business psyche; the male's is—and if you don't believe me now, read *Play Like a Man, Win Like a Woman* and see just how men have written all the rules of business, and why the rest of us need to learn them.

Because women think we have to succeed in the way men want us to, we have spent too much time looking in the wrong places: We keep trying to improve ourselves, we keep trying to reinvent ourselves, we keep learning more; we keep thinking if we try harder, somehow things will change.

Unfortunately, change hasn't happened. We do need to know the male rules of business. But we must also create and play by our own rules. We should be talking to each other; we should be planning with each other; we should be working to improve the situation for every one of us, not for just one of us. We should launch a new strategy to advance our careers as a whole, rather than advance our own careers at the expense of other women.

Few experts in the career-counseling area concern themselves with these ideas. In fact, they run contrary to what other businesswomen are currently telling their audiences— these people are still trying to solve our problems by recommending we play the boys' game better than the boys. Instead, it's time to make the case for creating a girls' game, for advancing as a group rather than as individuals. Because the truth is, women are a definable group, just like any other minority. And because we are, whether we are working for a company with a strong team environment or a weak one, women are always simultaneously working on another team, and that's the women's team.

This team cuts across the boundaries of business, ethnicity, age, and nationality. It's a reality for which there is no exception.

There's nothing wrong with tending your own desires. Women struggle so hard to figure out what we want. We know what our kids, our parents, and our husbands want; we even know what our dog wants, but we seldom have time to know what *we* want. We don't think it's right to be out there trying to fulfill our needs. We want to help others get theirs.

In the meantime, we hope that if we do all this, someone will notice us, and reward us. But the truth is: That isn't going to happen. The only way we win is to take care of ourselves. And that means taking care of other women too, because that's how we will all succeed—when we take care of each other.

Men like to say that there's no "us versus them" issue at the office. Then, too often, they go ahead and treat us as if we were a "them." We've all been in those situations where the work team suddenly seems to have left us out, or where we seem to get only so far before we feel frozen out by the men, or where we feel we must compete not just against our competitors at other companies, but against the few women at our level at our own company.

While we all recognize these predicaments, what we don't do is help each other deal with them.

I say: *The more we help each other, the more we all move toward greater success.*

Even more than that: *When we don't help each other, we all take a step backward.*

Our mantra has long been "I can do it." But this notion that we can accomplish our goals individually is antithetical to who we truly are. Our real mantra should be "*We* can do it."

Women will only make it if we make it together. One isolated success here or there won't do the trick. Only when we achieve a critical mass at the highest levels can we fully realize our potential at the office.

• • •

In the world of business, women have rarely operated as though supporting other women was an important part of the job. In fact, many of us have come to believe that another woman's gain is our own loss, and conversely that another woman's loss is our gain. Why? Because we are convinced that only a small number of executive slots are open to women. If that's really the case, then other women are the enemy—as anyone would feel while fighting for survival when resources are limited.

A young friend puts it succinctly: "As a woman, when I play the game of business, I always operate out of scarcity."

It's true that in the past many women have fought hard, and fought alone, to advance into certain rarefied positions. Therefore many of us have felt that we made it on our own, and that's the only way success should be achieved.

Women have also traditionally believed that speaking up too loudly for another woman, or for women's issues, can hurt us. What if that woman you recommended so highly performs poorly in the new job? What if the men begin to suspect that you are a secret feminist—couldn't this mortally wound your career?

No. Men feel safer around women who speak up for what they believe in—when it's appropriate. There is a big difference between expressing support for someone or something and beating others over the head with diatribes. When you demonstrate that your general ideals are greater than your personal ambition, you usually gain the admiration of both men and women.

Women have also been hesitant to give special treatment to other women for fear of being seen as Someone Who Favors Women. Singling out one individual for special attention can fly in the face of our image of ourselves as fair, objective people who don't play favorites.

But the guys mentor young men all the time. We all know who the boss's favorite is, and that he'll do anything he can for him. In fact, it's considered somewhat unusual if the boss *doesn't* have a protégé.

Some women who resent the fact that no male authority figure helped them because they were females respond by saying, "I don't want to lower myself to play that game. I want to help anyone at all who is deserving of my support."

I don't want you to stop helping deserving guys. I don't want you to feel like a bad person. I just want you to be willing to take care of other women. The boys are doing a great job of taking care of themselves already.

We need to identify the women around us who are comers and become integral to their success—and not worry that the men will attack us for playing the same game they do. Not long ago a young friend of mine quit her job at a weekly newsmagazine because she saw no chance for advancement. The senior male editor routinely gave the best assignments to his three favorite male reporters, but the top woman refused to do the same for the female reporters. When confronted, she explained, "That would be wrong." Perhaps, but the result is a magazine that can't hang on to its women because no one is willing to stick up for them.

Another issue: Many women want to play the game as though there were no differences between us and them. "Aren't we all equal?" they ask. As the statistics discussed earlier show, the answer is no—we're not equal in the business world.

In a recently released survey of women in finance conducted by Catalyst (the leading not-for-profit organization for female professionals), 65 percent of the women reported that they have to work harder than men to get the same rewards. A third of the women surveyed described the workplace as a hostile environment where sexist comments are tolerated and women are subjected to unwanted sexual advances. And only a fifth said that the opportunities to advance have increased greatly in the last five years. Many women cited exclusion from important networks as a barrier to their moving up.

"Every broker but me got invited to certain events," one executive woman told Catalyst, "so they all got input as to what they might be doing wrong or how they could improve their business. But not me." And several executive recruiters said one effect of the sluggish economy has been the decline in the position and status of women in corporate America.

Corroborating this perception are the dire predictions I recently heard from the women who invited me to speak to the female employees at a major financial firm—when times get hard, they said, the first people let go are always the women.

So although we are all just people, at work women are

not as equal as men. As observed by George Orwell in *Animal Farm*, "Some animals are more equal than others."

Furthermore, too often women accept the fact that the men will give us only so many openings at the top. After all, you keep the minorities down by keeping them separated. Give a little here and there, but let them kill each other.

How can you counterbalance that attitude? *Every woman who gets that one-and-only-female top job must be aware that half of her job, once she gets there, is to get another woman there too.*

A disproportionate number of women who have gotten close to the top have fallen in love with the idea of being that single special woman. There's no reason to abandon your team just because the other team has picked you out as an ally.

Rather than letting the men decide which woman gets the job, it makes more sense for the women to decide ahead of time whom to choose—and, once she gets there, to support her to make sure she does the job well.

When they wish to, women can and do work very well together. For example, Carol, a very successful friend, started receiving signals that her department was about to undergo significant budget cuts. Much of her staff, many of them women she had hired, would be let go. Carol herself was in jeopardy.

One day Carol called and asked for my advice. I knew her job was in danger, but I also knew she'd have no problem finding another great position. I told her that, given her talents, her next job should be running her own company. Since Carol was woman friendly and hired more women than her male counterparts, I knew this would benefit not only her, but all of us.

I had just heard that a CEO position was about to open up, and I, along with Carol's other allies, suspected she would be perfect for it. But we all knew that landing this job would require intense and careful politicking, so we had to plan carefully. First, we compiled a list of the most important women each of us knew who could influence the company's board, and we made sure that everyone on the list received a phone call. We then checked to see which search firm would be handling the position, and when we discovered it was one where we knew one of the female partners, we enlisted her in the battle too.

When Carol became one of three people being considered seriously, we increased the pressure, enlisting at least a dozen more women to help. The campaign worked. Carol landed the job, and today she is one of the most powerful women in her field.

This isn't to say that sometimes these ideas don't backfire. They do. I once knew some women at a midsize Southern California company who began meeting regularly and sharing knowledge. They thought they had a powerful group going that would advance all their careers.

After two years, one of the women was laid off. The other women, knowing how smart she was, found the firing unfair and were incensed. Feeling their power as a group of successful executives, they thought they could right a wrong.

What they didn't do was stop to ask a million and one questions. Why had the woman been laid off? Was there trouble in her department? Were there financial pressures? What was the real story? These women didn't do the research. Instead, they organized a quick protest, they made their opinions known both inside and outside the company, and they received some bad media coverage the company did not want.

Soon these women were called in by their bosses, who told them they didn't understand the specifics of the situation, and then read them the riot act. If they couldn't do the appropriate fact-finding work, they should have gone to their bosses and asked them for the real story. In other words, true team players would have kept the company's concerns in mind.

None of the women was fired, but the incident put a damper on the group. Feeling humbled, the women returned to their corners to try to make up the territory they'd lost with their bosses.

When one of the women in this group told me of their woes, I urged her not to give up. Life isn't always fair, I said. The woman in question was good, the rest of you protested, you landed in trouble, and that's the way of the world. It doesn't mean you should stop organizing. It just means you need to do your homework next time.

The moral: Being on the women's team isn't always about changing the world or righting all wrongs. It's about working with other women to become smarter and more successful. When you're smart, not only do you know the rules of the game, and the best strategies, but you keep in mind all the other games taking place around you.

• • •

If this is as obvious as it seems, why haven't women been playing on the same team?

Perhaps the main reason is that too many of us have been looking to the men to give us that power. The other night, at a dinner with a lawyer who's also a former member of Congress, I talked about the troubles businesswomen face. The man was skeptical. I then asked him what percentage of partners in law firms, and general counsels in corporate America, were female.

After thinking it over, the man guessed that 30 percent of partners and 40 percent of general counsels were women.

"Wrong," I said. "It's 12 percent for each."

We then landed in a discussion about how women got the right to vote. He said it happened because the men eventually decided it was the right course of action. I disagreed, saying female suffrage was achieved only when significant numbers of women, many of them married to important men, took to the streets to protest their disenfranchisement. (The final passing vote supposedly came from a politician whose wife used her powers in the bedroom to sway his mind.)

Women would never have gotten the right to vote if they'd waited for the men to give it to them. They got it because they fought so hard and exerted so much pressure that the men were forced to capitulate.

Likewise, working women today have spent far too much time sitting in the office saying, "It's not fair," or "I deserve more," or "They should recognize me."

We seem to feel that if we repeat these complaints often enough, the men will wake up one day and say, "Hey, these girls really are entitled to more power."

That's not going to happen.

No one gives power away. You only get power if you usurp it. People *take* power. That's the phrase you hear throughout history—people taking power. You don't hear about people waiting for power to be given them. You don't hear about people being surprised with the gift of power. Change is not brought on by a group of people sitting around waiting for change to happen.

In my last book I talked about a dismal word called "hope." This word is unempowering. It allows us to believe that we're taking action when we're actually taking no action at all— we're just being passive.

A better word is "want." Don't say, "I hope to be promoted." Say, "I want to be promoted."

Similarly we shouldn't be saying, "I hope things change for women." We should say, "I want things to change." (And, of course, "I'm going to make those changes occur.")

Here are more reasons why we're not yet on the same team:

Even as we enter the twenty-first century, society remains ambivalent about supporting women at the office. Yes, women constitute almost half the work force, and everyone pays lip service to the fact that the economy needs all these workers. But the underlying messages aren't clear. Family and children are still felt to be a woman's responsibility, and if problems arise there, it's the woman's fault. Therefore, if she's at work, she's not truly fulfilling her obligations.

My proof: If society really believed women should be working alongside the men, good day care would be universal. The government, fully behind the idea that women should be in the workplace, would guarantee that our children are well cared for while the women are at work. But the government doesn't force anyone to provide day care, and we don't have government-run day-care centers (unless, of course, you actually work for the government).

Such ambivalence about women in the workplace means that we'll have a tougher time getting the team together because we're not convinced we even belong on the team. Do we want powerful women executives? Do we want real business success? As long as we're not sure about entering teams, we'll have a hard time forming them.

Another reason: We don't have good role models for a women's team. That first group of successful women were taught that the only road to success was to be more of a man than the men. Therefore, they tried to join the men's team. Furthermore, not only didn't these women think about the women's team, there weren't enough women to even create a team. So today, when we look around for team role models in business, we see few. It is our task to ensure the next generation will have it much easier.

(Whenever I think about that first group of women, Margaret Thatcher comes to mind. She may have provided a good role model for success, but she did little to help other women. She was too busy trying to succeed in the role of a man.)

Women also question the very objective of the word *team*—we see the rewards they offer and many of us aren't interested. We don't want to be the typical male boss who routinely fires subordinates, maltreats workers, and is a slave to the company and the stockholders. We don't want all the money and the perks. We'd rather see a prize of a more balanced workplace or a better lifestyle. So why play on a team when you don't covet the reward?

This is why so many women quit before making it to the top, something that just happened to an electronic-business executive vice president I know. This woman was an almost unanimous choice to become her division's new president—everyone from the conglomerate's CEO to her staff assumed the job was hers. But she surprised everyone by taking early retirement. Why? She looked at what the company wanted from her and she knew that although she'd do a great job, she'd be miserable doing it. She had worked hard and done well. But the big prize—one very much made in the male image—made her realize that what she really wanted was her own life back. She resigned, and she's never been happier.

Of course, another major reason why women haven't formed teams is that we're simply not used to them. Boys grow up understanding how teams work; they play on them naturally because the model of a team is a masculine one. Little girls are taught to play individually—we're brought up to shine through being unique. We spend the rest of our lives wanting to be as different as possible so we can stand out as individuals. Otherwise we fear the loss of our femininity.

Society is only now becoming familiar and comfortable with the notion of women's teams. For example, the American soccer team that won the last World Cup was a wonderful example of female teamwork. But I can still remember the startled reaction of the television announcers (as well as many others) when they discovered that some of those girls were attractive, as though being on a team and being pretty was an oxymoron. Then, when these women had babies, the result was shock. I recall a male executive at CNN telling me, "My God, that girl has a husband and a baby and she's a halfback!"

Women also shy away from teams because we think that, to be on a team, you must have a relationship with everyone on it, and a positive one at that. But on a team, it's fine to have a good relationship with some people and not with others. Your commitment is to the team, not to its every member. Too many women tell me they won't join a certain team because they don't like this or that woman—"I can't stand Janice and I'd never be on the same team." But you don't have to like everyone. Just like the team.

The truth is, even the relationships that aren't good can help you. In her book *Odd Girl Out*, Rachel Simmons points out that you can and should have conflict and care in the same relationship. There's much to be learned from the conflict, as girls need to learn that a balanced relationship is one in which "care and conflict are comfortably exchanged."

• • •

Still one more reason why women haven't succeeded in business as predicted by all the experts in the last few decades: We have been playing the game the wrong way, i.e., the man's way.

Study after study shows that women tend to be more relationship-oriented than men. We are constantly striving for, and constantly involved in, relationships. That's the way we achieve power, strength, and love—through interaction with other people. No matter what the situation, whether it involves our dry cleaner or our stockbroker or our boss, we're more likely to view the other person as just that—a person—rather than another party in an impersonal transaction.

These same studies show we are more likely than men to make, and keep, close friends, at home or at work. In this new age of business, where maintaining and servicing clients is so important, our predisposition to forming strong relationships should work to our advantage. A talent for working with people means we can make them feel comfortable and earn their trust, and that we're probably good listeners.

Yet we have forgotten this as we struggle to rise to the top. Instead of playing the game in the relationship-oriented manner in which we're most comfortable and have the most talent, we've been acting as though each one of us were on a separate team, fighting only for ourselves in that very macho male way.

Let's take back the word *team* from the men. In its best sense, *team* is a relationship-oriented word. When women are willing to work on a team together, we'll all do better. That's what a team is for.

• • •

The final reason to join the team: We've tried everything else. We've followed what every get-ahead book, every career coach, and every business consultant has told us for the last twenty years. And it's all failed.

Many women who feel frustrated by corporate America have left it to start a business of their own. The good news is that as of 2000, nearly 40 percent of all the businesses in America were female owned.

But here's the bad news: Such businesses have the same access to traditional financing as women have to the inner power circles of corporate America, i.e., these women end up with approximately 12 percent of the traditional venture capital money.

It doesn't matter where you are—corporate business, education, or law. It doesn't matter whether you work for the largest company on the Fortune 500, you're a freelance journalist, or you own your own business. We women are stuck.

It's time to stop doing it as individuals and do it together. By working on the same team we will find ways to attain our fair share of power and impact the system. Eventually we'll reach a point where we won't feel we have to work twice as hard as the guys to achieve the same reward.

Just as the right to vote and the right to own property didn't come until we demanded it, equal access to capital and the inner circles of power will not come until we are a united force.

Join the women's team. Whether you like it or not, as far as the men are concerned, if you were born with XX chromosomes, you're already on it. It doesn't matter whether you work for a large corporation or you're a one-woman shop. You might as well become an active player. You may be surprised by all the rewards you will reap.

Many of these bonuses (as you will discover in the next chapters) will take place at the office: For example, the more we work in teams, the more we'll be able to take risks. Instead of entering meetings as three individual women who are lone islands, we will go in knowing we have support, and if one of us sags, the others can chip in.

We won't be so alone all the time; we will have more help—one of the team's prime functions is to make sure each of its members is doing well. You'll always have someone to confide in, as well as a wider net of resources to turn to as situations warrant.

Here are other rewards: If you join the team, you're more likely to be noticed at the office—the other women at your organizational meetings take note of anyone who is smart. You'll make more contacts, both at your workplace and within your chosen profession. You'll have support when you're faced with failure, and just as importantly, when you're successful (and yes, currently women are less likely to support you when you're doing well). You'll have help doing anything you want to do, instead of thinking you have to do it all alone. You'll learn more about your company, because you'll be hearing about issues and people in areas that you might not otherwise have any contact with. And, instead of wondering whom you can trust (or if there's anyone you can trust at all), you'll develop relationships where you work together unquestioningly.

You'll also find plenty of rewards outside your job. You'll bring balance into your life, making both home and business less stressful. Maybe your team will create a baby-sitting cooperative at the office, or maybe it will invent new opportunities for part-time work, such as flextime or job sharing, so you can see your family more often.

Some years ago a CNN executive producer had to move to another state when her husband was transferred. The company's first instinct was to replace her, but I knew she was the best person for the job and that she could do it just as well from her new home. Why not give her a chance? I doubt a man (particularly at that time) would have considered this. But another woman could understand that this producer needed to follow her husband, even though her own job was important. I also knew that this woman was a perfectionist and wasn't going to use this opportunity to relax and work less. If anything, she would work even harder to prove herself—and, if she couldn't do it, she'd be the first to say so. Indeed, the former, not the latter, took place.

The team will make your life more fun. Rather than thinking of all your problems as the end of the world, you'll feel lighter because you have more support. Instead of considering every woman potential competition, you'll see potential teammates and friends. You can have a baby shower where everyone in the room feels good about each other; you can meet the new women knowing they're on your side rather than their own.

You'll feel less stress. When women are supportive of each other, we find strategies to help each other solve problems. And as women become the bosses in major companies, we'll create systems friendly to everyone, especially families.

Finally, we'll be able to forge some real changes in society. Once women see themselves as able to work together in powerful teams, we will bring that power to bear not just in our little companies or in our little village, but in the world—on subjects that concern us, such as education or the environment.

I know one group of women in California whose local city councilman was unresponsive to their neighborhood's needs. A career politician, supported by the town's big business interests, the man couldn't have cared less about school crossings or potholes.

One night these women were talking generally about how poorly they were being represented, and specifically about speed bumps, which they needed to slow down all the fast drivers on their streets. One of the women, Kristen, was clearly leading the discussion, and so the others, who very much believed in the women's team, had an idea. Kristen should run for city council herself. Many of these women had been successful in making their companies more female friendly. Why not try their city, too?

Kristen's eyes lit up, but could it be done? The councilman was ensconced in the local power structure. Still, the idea was so inviting that she consented, and soon the women were enlisting everyone in the neighborhood sympathetic to the cause, even putting their kids to work, dressing them up in T-shirts emblazoned with Kristen's name and asking them to walk around the malls, signing up names and collecting money.

Running on a platform that the councilman wasn't responding to the needs of women and families, Kristen won her election. She went on to serve several terms on the city council.

Once we begin to work together, and we achieve real victories, we will all be able to feel our power, just as the boys feel theirs. We won't feel like victims. We will bring the attitude of being a winner over from the office to any part of our life we wish. When that happens, the world will change in many innovative ways.

2
How to Join the Team

One detail that highlights the difference between men and women involves how the two sexes found their first job. Most women will tell you they applied for a zillion positions to land one good interview. Men have other ways of getting their foot in the door.

For example, Gary and Tracy are honchos at a large Midwestern advertising concern. They both started working two decades ago at a time when entry level jobs were difficult to find. How did Tracy get her job? A native New Englander, she sent a letter to almost every major advertising company in the country, and got responses from only a few. The only company that would hire her (as what they called a secretary-assistant) was in Chicago. She didn't want to move (although now she loves it). She didn't have much choice.

Gary graduated from the University of Illinois and immediately set his sights on the firm. Through networking, he discovered that one of the firm's partners had also belonged to his college fraternity. He applied for a position and within a week a job was his.

To the company's credit, Gary and Tracy spent an equal amount of time getting to their current positions. But if you asked Tracy (and I did), she claims that she had to work much harder than Gary, who once left the firm to join another company, which then went under after a year.

Today's business system is, as always, geared toward rewarding the boss's frat brother's son, or the golfer who plays in the foursome with the chairman of the board, or the guy who was the captain of the senior executive vice president's son's college tennis team. There's no getting around the fact that although recently women have started having an easier time getting the entry-level jobs, and even the midlevel jobs, it's much harder for a woman to be picked for the top jobs. The scrutiny is greater before she gets picked, and remains greater ever after.

Women have to start playing the game in a way that will level the playing field. We don't have the frat-house connections, the drinking pals, or the football game buddies. We're not as likely to be out there for that after-work drink, or the casual dinner on Tuesday night, or the hockey game. Therefore we have to find some way to match these opportunities. Whether you intend a career at a large corporation or you want to work alone, we all have to form the teams that become our equivalent of those old boy networks.

• • •

The first step is to overcome your fears about being on a team.

- **Fear:** If you join that women's company-wide organization, you'll be seen as an old-fashioned feminista.
- **Reality:** Here's a shocker: *Feminist* isn't an ugly word. Women have allowed men to define too many words for us, such as *aggressive*, which the men use to describe us in an unpleasant way, while saving the favorable connotations for themselves. An aggressive male is a real go-getter; an aggressive female is a bitch.

Feminism is another one. The men use it with negative implications—and we women have bought into their interpretation. But what is its actual definition? According to my *Webster's New World Dictionary*: "the principle that women should have political, economic, and social rights equal to those of men."

Can anyone really disagree with that? Feminism doesn't mean bra-burning. It means fairness. So you can either buy the mean-spirited definition of a ball-buster who wants more than she deserves, or you can accept the dictionary's definition.

- **Fear:** By joining the women's team, you will have to sacrifice your individuality.
- **Reality:** Being on a team does not mean that you will become invisible. Nor that you will turn into a robot. Every team has a star. It also has its most creative person, its most humorous, and its most talented. The team is made up of individuals, not anonymous characters.

Women like to think of themselves as unique, interesting, and unusual. These qualities make us attractive to our partners and to the world. Being a team player doesn't mean giving up these attributes. Instead, you can become a better version of you. Each member of the team brings her own talents to bear; you can even improve yours by taking advantage of all the talents around you.

- *Fear:* The idea of being on a team scares you.
- *Reality:* Maybe what really bothers you is the male definition of the word *team*. But women can form teams our own way.

The male team: A bunch of guys who play a game that has clear, unqualified rules. They're shown the goalpost, the one that says "win," and they go for it. This team has a leader who commands through strict rules that don't accommodate individuality or shifting situations. You are told everything from how to dress to how to win, and the sole focus is victory.

The female team is concerned with the win, too, but it's also concerned with understanding the importance of that win. It's not as much about making the great sale as forming the great relationship. It emphasizes unity rather than stars. And if this sounds slightly unclear, that's because the concept of a woman's team is harder to express—it's still being determined. All of us have a chance to help define the word as we create the teams that will make us successful.

Anyway, whether you like the idea of teams or not, you're already playing on at least one team, the company team. You're also playing on that second team, the women's team. So you might as well get used to the team, and use it to your advantage.

- *Fear:* If women spend our time working for and thinking about other women, we will become ghettoized.
- *Reality:* Anything we can do to get other women more work, and therefore more exposure, is helpful.

I once created a daytime talk show called *CNN & Co.*, which was designed to let women discuss significant issues of the day, from peace in the Middle East to home education, instead of the standard you-and-your-uterus women's afternoon television fodder.

Most of the men loved the idea and gave it a green light. It was the women in the CNN newsroom who panicked. Why? Because they were afraid the show would take women out of the main discussion and lock them in this one half-hour program. These women gave me nothing but negative feedback. (Because the format resembled the old *Hollywood Squares* set, they even helped create a killer nickname for the show, "Bitches in Boxes.")

My point was that CNN was on-air twenty-four hours a day, and instead of seeing white men for that entire time, we would now see them for only twenty-three and a half hours. I was also convinced that some of the women on the show would start to appear in other venues, once people saw how articulate and smart they were.

The show worked, not only because it got good ratings, but because the women proved they could talk about important issues. Equally importantly, when these women returned to their offices after their show was broadcast, they often had up to a dozen phone calls from producers asking them to appear on other media, which was under pressure to show diversity. Instead of ghettoizing women, the show helped create media stars.

- *Fear:* There isn't enough time to do your work and join the team.
- *Reality:* Women often won't go out and have that after-work drink with the guys because they say they don't have enough time. There's so much to do at the office, there's so much to do at home, and it all has to be done just right. Who has time for anything else?

You do.

I'm not telling you to go guzzle a half dozen beers with the boys every evening. But you can't hole up in your office all the time. You can't keep saying, "I come here to get my work done, and a drink isn't work."

Yes, it is work! Lunch with the women from different departments is work. Breakfast with your partner on a new project and her best friend from a competing outfit is work. This type of socializing is where you begin to build a knowledge base about your company and your competitors. It's how you begin to create your own equivalent of a golf foursome.

You think the guys on the fairway spend all their time talking about the deal? Most of their time is spent talking about the Rams' chances of beating the Raiders. More important than the actual words is the relationship-building as the guys feel each other out, see who they can get along with, discover who shares their goals.

This type of socializing is a completely legitimate form of work.

- *Fear:* If you build relationships with other women hoping that you will profit from them some day, you are being manipulative.

- *Reality:* You don't mind talking with other women at the day-care center about the best new pediatrician in town or the best deals on diapers. And whom do you listen to? To the woman who dresses her kid the way you want to dress yours, or the woman who seems most like you. How do you find a good dentist? You don't do it by looking in the phone book. You do it by word of mouth, by seeing, by networking.

We get information about these things all the time from our networks, except at work, where we back down because here we think we're supposed to make it entirely on our own.

Women are struggling with this concept because we think that using a friend to achieve some positive result in business is nasty, immoral, and manipulative. We don't understand that having a close friend help you make a business contact is a routine favor that men do for each other all the time. After all, if we're sick, we expect our best friend to show up at the hospital when we need company; we have no moral qualms about that. Why should we feel uncomfortable about asking her to introduce us to a business associate who could help us? If your friend manufactures baseball caps, and your company wants to create a promotion using caps, it's not unreasonable to ask her for help. Yet somehow we're not comfortable with that, as though friendships are violated if we tap them to meet our professional needs, even when we're comfortable using them for personal ones. It's time to get over that guilt. (We also have to get over our fear of being rejected when we ask for help. It's okay to ask the question and receive a negative response. She's not saying no to your entire friendship. She's just not keen on this particular request. Move on.)

• • •

There are two primary ways to join the women's team—*formal* and *informal* (which you can join both inside and outside your company).

The difference between the two is simple. The formal teams are organizations sanctioned by some authority, with a structure, bylaws, and some sort of oversight. For instance, General Electric runs a program called the Women Helping Women Awards; the company also sponsors a Women of Color conference. The accounting firm Deloitte & Touche sponsors a "Women's Initiative" for the retention and advancement of women. Bayer Women: Leaders for the Global Marketplace provides women and people of color at the drug company with the critical skills necessary to advance to senior positions throughout the world. Boeing's Women in Leadership has chapters in cities where the aircraft manufacturer has large numbers of employees, and has, as one of its network features, mentoring opportunities for members to consult with executives.

The informal teams are exactly what you'd think—more informal. These networks comprise the women with whom you lunch once a month, or the women whose children are in your kids' nursery school. These teams have no real authority, their structure is more fluid, and they seldom have bylaws. If you're a freelancer, or you work at a very small company, they may be your only option.

The traditional formal network is usually created because the women's interests and the company's interests coincide. The women want to meet each other and learn how to network in the company, as well as to advance in it. The corporation has a stake in getting to know its female staff better in order to identify potential leaders for promotion.

If your company doesn't have a formal network, start one. Be that woman with the great idea. Most of these networks are begun by a woman who realized an opportunity to make a name for herself, and who provided an opportunity for other women to advance.

However, it's hard to start all by yourself; you'll probably need to find a few like-minded colleagues. As you begin, have a focused discussion about your purposes. Be clear about what you want to achieve.

Maybe you want to find women within the company who can mentor you, or women you can mentor. Maybe you want to learn more about the roadblocks other women have faced at your firm, as well as their successes. Perhaps you want to get to know women in other divisions in order to broaden your professional contacts, or you want to discuss issues as far ranging as children or continuing education. Perhaps you want to expand your friendships beyond the small group in your office, or develop a support group, or learn more about leadership.

You also need to decide the membership requirements of your network.

Part of your preliminary discussion should be: What are the parameters of this network? Is it a broad, inclusive group that all the women in the company (and even the men) can join, or is it focused more specifically on women who have achieved some professional level—say, the account-manager level and up? You must decide this in the beginning. Each type of network is different.

One of the most effective specialized networks I've ever encountered was set up by the late Dee Woods, the former executive secretary of CNN founder Ted Turner (and who eventually became a senior vice president). Called Tessie, which roughly stood for Turner Executive Secretaries, it was a network of executive secretaries who got to know each other, shared information, and were able to move the action better for themselves and their bosses. Every year the network members went away on a retreat, not long after the one taken by the major executives. They generally even went to the same town as their bosses, but instead of flying first class and staying in an expensive hotel, they went tourist and found more reasonably priced lodgings. Yet, despite its modest finances, this was a very powerful group.

Dee founded the network with the clear vision that it should be only for secretaries who had been at the company for at least a year. She knew exactly what she wanted to achieve, and she achieved it.

If your company has an effective human resources department, your next step is to enroll it.

This is the best way to get the company to support your plan. You and your members will need ways to communicate with each other, places to meet, permission to leave your job to go to an event. You'll also require someone who can take the time to keep your records.

Having the stamp of human resources is important. However, a caveat: The minute you take your idea to human resources, it takes on the company's patina. Human resources doesn't operate anything that isn't in the best interest of the company, and their goal will be to shape the network in such a way that it helps the corporation. This can be fine, however, as your network will help the company identify whom among the women to advance, and how to make it happen.

This said, you must be careful when you approach the human resources people (and thus senior management). Creating advancement for women is something human resources should already be doing. If you come armed with complaints, someone in human resources will be threatened.

Remember: In almost every human resources department there are wonderful, warm people, and there are corporate sellouts. Be a smart player. Avoid the latter, and look for someone who's sympathetic. Enlist her on your team. Likewise, if you know there's a like-minded female executive in the higher echelons of the company, go to her and tell her what you want to do as well. (But don't forget you still must include human resources in your plan.)

Also: You must be reasonably sophisticated about your company, the culture, the attitude toward women, and how the top executives will react. You don't need to worry about anyone saying your idea is stupid. You do need to know if the culture is flexible. Has your company shown any interest in diversity or everyday issues such as day care? What are the obstacles you're likely to face?

If you think human resources will be less than enthusiastic about your ideas, research networks in other companies so that when you have your first meeting, you can support your idea with solid evidence. Show that you know the percentages of female employees in the company, as well as how many are single and how many have children; if applicable, know the percentage of your customers who are women. Make the argument that empowering women is good for your business.

Let's say you work for a plastics company. That plastic ends up somewhere, whether it's in containers that eventually go to Rubbermaid or in children's toys or anything in between. There is a good business case to be made as to why more women should be included in the final decisions about plastics—a woman's point of view will help the company market its wares better.

It's almost impossible not to make a case that it's good for any business to appear more female friendly. For example, look at the corporate turnover rate. Women are leaving in droves from companies that don't support them. In fact, 1,600 women become new business owners every single day. According to the Small Business Administration, that's twice the rate of male-owned businesses. As mentioned, smart women who don't get promoted start their own businesses and often end up as your company's competitors.

Proposing that your company support a women's network is an opportunity for you to show your brains and your skills. You are making your employer a business proposition, and you need to approach it as such. Outline your objectives, how you will present the case to the company, how much it will cost them. Be prepared to explain why it's in their best interest (and the best interest of the employees). You must also be aware that as great as your idea is, you will meet some resistance. Someone might say that the men don't have a men's network, so why should the women? In short, you must prepare to answer any and all objections.

Besides thoroughly assessing the human resources people, who speak for the corporate hierarchy, find out how key individuals in the company (including your boss) feel about your plan to start a women's network. You probably need at least some of the senior women in the company on your side.

Be a scout. Talk to the people who know the company best, from the secretaries up to the big bosses. Does your company simply pay lip service to diversity, or are they serious but haven't figured out how to implement it?

When forming a formal network at your company, remember that your company is going to be more than an equal partner once they get involved.

Just because the company supports you doesn't mean that it won't bring its own needs into play. This is not like starting a group in which you're the one and only leader. It now takes on a dual mission, yours and the company's. It will take a new form and shape, and your ideas may now have to be approved by higher management. Your agenda may be to achieve 50 percent parity for women in the company, or to start a mentoring program. The company's agenda may be to prevent discrimination lawsuits from female employees, or to put on a better public face, vis-à-vis diversity.

The company may also decide to change your membership criteria. Perhaps they'll want you to invite all the female employees, whereas you only wanted women above, or below, a certain level. The company may want total inclusion and insist that men must be allowed to join. They may insist that certain senior-level executives be present at all meetings, whereas you were hoping for privacy. After all, different words are spoken when bosses are around.

Once the network is formed, anything can happen. At one company the African-American women felt the women's network didn't fully suit their purposes and they formed their own. The Latina women then decided they wanted one too. The original founders, who were mostly white, couldn't understand why the women couldn't all do it together—just as the company didn't understand why they couldn't all do it together as employees.

In other words, the picture you formed in your mind when you were lying in bed one night dreaming about your network may not resemble what comes to be. But starting a group like this isn't only about your fantasy. It's also about reality. There are a million and one possible permutations. Some are great. Some aren't. You must learn to live with most of them.

A final caveat: Make sure you don't get so caught up in the excitement of this project that you stop paying attention to your real job. Unless starting this network is what you want to do full-time (and such possibilities exist), don't let it succeed at the expense of your job. For almost all of us, this is an adjunct to a career. You don't become CEO from running a network (although the network itself can help you become so visible that some day you become CEO).

If a network already exists, there's only one step to take. Join it.

Whether it's good, bad, or indifferent, get involved. Opportunities abound, even if you don't like the people who run it or the programs that are offered. Great things can still happen.

An example: At one large conglomerate, most of the female executives worked hard to create a strong woman's organization. The men tolerated the group but didn't pay much heed until one of the women, Vanessa, ran into trouble.

Vanessa had discovered that she was making less than her male counterpart for doing the same job. When she confronted her boss, he freely admitted that she was correct, but justified the difference by saying that, in fact, most of the women throughout the entire company earned less than the men.

The women's group discussed the problem and issued a private, in-house ultimatum: Management had to address the issue of women's salaries. If they were found to be unfairly low, they had to be brought to parity. Otherwise the women would take the issue public and, if necessary, they would resign.

While the men weren't sure if the women were bluffing, they decided not to take the chance (particularly after the corporate counsel warned the CEO that the company was leaving itself wide open to a class action lawsuit).

The result: A committee was formed to analyze the company's pay structure, and eventually many of the women were given raises commensurate with the men's salaries.

More benefits of networks: You get to meet the more senior women in the company. You can be seen by a number of people in a position to help your career. I've never heard of a company where a reasonable number of the female executives didn't participate, unless they were specifically asked not to join.

Anyone and everyone you meet through the network broadens your professional base. You hear about possibilities, personalities, and problems. Maybe you'll sit at the table with three women in corporate public relations, and they'll talk about the guy in the West Coast office who's impossible to work for, or the woman in Boston who's a dream, or the cutbacks that are coming. Knowing the problems in the mail room because you met the woman who runs the department may not seem valuable at the moment, but the more information you have about your company, the better an employee you will be—and the more intelligently you will be able to maneuver and strategize your own career.

In networking, quantity is as important as quality. It's great if you're part of a tiny network of immensely powerful people, but few of us ever get to that place. It's more likely that you will need to make many acquaintances so that, when you require help some time in the future, you won't just have five people in your corner who might be there for you—you'll have fifty.

An admonition: Just as getting a network off the ground should not monopolize your attention, don't fall into the trap of believing that the women's network is the sole answer to your career. It's not. It's a vehicle that gets you noticed and considered. Use it effectively. Tell yourself, "I am here for a business purpose, and that is to network. Therefore I need to operate in the meeting to achieve those ends." Come in, look around, and sit down next to someone you've never seen before. This is an opportunity to meet new people. Don't spend your time with your old friends. That's not networking. Networking is making conversation with strangers.

I know one company that arranges monthly luncheons for its women's network and assigns seats via a computer to make sure no one sits next to a woman she's sat next to before. The women are forced to mix it up. (And they're not allowed to run around and switch tables, either.)

Be a participant. Don't stand on the periphery. Yes, it is difficult to walk into a room of strangers who all seem to know each other. The greatest rewards come from conquering difficult situations. Step out of your comfort zone and ask questions, or linger behind to introduce yourself to the speaker.

Have fun. Fun! Networks don't have to be strictly business. They can also be seen as an opportunity to let your hair down, a place where you can find out you're not as off-the-mark as you thought. Listen to other women tell stories similar to yours. Find out how they coped. So often these stories are funny. Laugh with them.

You can use these teams many ways. If you're having a specific problem in your department, you may be able to talk to other women at your table about how to deal with it without violating confidentiality.

Recently, after a speech, a woman asked me a question about her boss, a difficult man who assigned her tasks that didn't correspond with the company's vision. Meanwhile, she had become friendly with her boss's boss, whom she liked enormously. But her firm's structure made it difficult for her to talk to anyone over her boss's head. What should she do?

That's what I call a "stuck" question—she's stuck in a bad place. She can't tell her own boss she thinks he's stupid. She can't ask her best friend or her cousin; their only intelligent answer is "I can't really help." But if she were at a women's network lunch, she could pose the question and learn how others at her company dealt with such an issue.

Another plus: Most networks invite the big boss a few times a year to talk about goals, budgets, and other subjects you might never know about if you weren't in the network.

These networks also give you a chance to observe up close the kinds of women who succeed in your company, giving you the opportunity to see if you could fit in with the prevailing model.

For example, the successful women within Turner Broadcasting may have looked different from one another, and had different skills, but we shared certain fundamental traits. We were all activists, we had senses of humor, we were comfortable in our own space, and we didn't take crap from anyone. The men in our corporation were unconventional entrepreneurial types who didn't care much about clothes but did care about big ideas, taking risks, and having a good time. Clearly they liked to hire and promote women like us because they felt at ease around us. (This should hardly be a surprise, as everyone tends to hire the people with whom they feel most relaxed.)

If you saw the most successful women at IBM fifteen years ago, they probably all looked like the men, wearing dark blue suits and white shirts and carrying attaché cases. Most big companies have a prototype of the kind of woman who makes it versus the kind who doesn't. If you are part of a network, you will see what the successful women at your company look like—not just how they dress and how they talk, but who they really are. That's consequential information.

Finally: Go to as many network-sponsored programs and lectures as possible. The subject doesn't matter. You might think that you're not interested in better forms of accounting or seemingly arcane legal issues. But you never know what little gems you might pick up. Personally, I've never attended a program where I didn't learn something or walk away with a new idea or a new contact.

• • •

Something to consider: Just because a company sponsors a network doesn't mean that it is committed to real change.

I recently gave the keynote address for a division of a Fortune 500 conglomerate. Normally these speeches are pro forma—at some point a company representative calls me, we have a brief chat about the speech's subject matter, I give the speech, and that's the end of that.

The representatives (there were several) from this company called to tell me that my speech was to be part of their annual women's diversity day. And indeed they did want to celebrate their women. But because they were afraid that the men might feel uncomfortable and see the occasion as an "us against them" situation, the company had invited the men, too. And, I was told by the representatives, I wasn't allowed to say anything that might offend the men. And, I had to let the company see a copy of everything I was going to say before I could say it.

Frankly, this company bordered on the absurd. Various people telephoned me repeatedly, wasting time and energy, relentlessly talking about what could and what couldn't be spoken aloud. They finally gave me the ultimate warning—I wasn't to say anything that anyone at all might find in any way controversial.

I argued back, saying that issues can't be addressed without some degree of confrontation. If all you ever give are happy, self-congratulatory speeches, nothing changes.

After a while it became clear to me that the move this company was making was akin to a baby step: a little bitty change to make the place look more female friendly. The company was well meaning, but because they lacked a true commitment to diversity, the network would probably be unproductive.

Another issue: Last month I gave the keynote at a women's leadership network at another Fortune 500 company. This group started off women-only, but over time the company felt pressured to include men, believing that if the organization was truly about diversity, no one should feel left out.

As a result, white men composed a third of the room. I had no idea why I was talking to them. I love men, but my goal is not to inspire white men to do better. My message is quite different. But my immediate object is to keep the whole audience engaged, which meant diluting the female message I had intended to impart.

The speech was fine (although much of the passion had been taken out). I talked the requisite hour and then asked for questions. Normally there are dozens. Here there were hardly any. Yet I sensed most of the audience was with me.

After a break, I was scheduled for another panel. But on my way to the ladies' room I was bombarded by women grabbing me for advice and taking me aside for confidences. I asked one of them why she hadn't raised her questions after the speech. Before she could respond, another woman said, "Oh, that's because John Jones was sitting right behind us, and he would have known too much about what we were asking." One after another the women told me that they had pressing issues they wanted addressed, but they were afraid to mention them when the men were present.

Here was a company that thought it was empowering women by forming a network but, by including men, had established a program attended by several hundred hesitant women. The company was trying to do its best, but it hadn't really created a team that served the women's needs.

• • •

Let's say you're already on the formal team, but you want to join an *informal team* too. If none exist around you, what do you do?

The same as if there were no formal team. Start one. Use the tactics described above. Look for like-minded women, ones who care about the same issues you do, and who care about other women. We all hear about such women constantly. They work in other departments as well as in our own; we are introduced to them at meetings, we hear about them while talking around the office cooler. Pay attention.

Assume you can be helped by people on all levels—on the

executive floor or among that smart group of assistants be-low you. Careers shift and slide. Today's trainees may be to-morrow's CEOs.

Once you've started to identify likely candidates for your informal team, the next step is: Get out of your hole.

Getting to know people within the company is as much a part of our careers as getting a specific job done. As men-tioned, too often the women are the ones who eat lunch at their desks and who are too busy to have drinks after work. Get it into your head that a meal with five female colleagues is an important part of the job.

A simple way to start: Find a small group of women and have lunch with them on a regular basis. Look around the of-fice for women who seem interesting and who might have something to contribute. Take the risk of saying, "I think it would be fun for some of us to get together once a week. We can have lunch and brainstorm and get to know each other better." That woman in legal whom you dealt with last week—she seems smart and nice. Send her an e-mail and say, "Five of us have started doing a regular Thursday lunch. Please join us—it'll be fun."

Keep in mind: For some, dinner can sound intimidating. It feels as though it infringes on private time. Breakfast, lunch, or drinks is a better idea.

If you're uncomfortable being so bold, have lunch with two friends and say, "Why don't we do this every month? Each of us can invite someone different within the company so we get to know more people." Or each of you could invite someone in a related business field who's outside the com-pany. Either way works.

Point: When you begin to set up a team, be open-minded. A lot of women are burdened with unfair reputations. Unless you truly know otherwise, assume that any woman wants to help herself and other women get ahead. Don't refuse to make initial contact because you've heard some bad news. Sometimes this gossip is wrong. Maybe no one's ever asked her to join any group at all. Maybe she's shy. (At the same time, if you know someone is uncomfortable supporting women's issues, don't include her at the beginning stages of your planning meeting. You may end up spending valuable time and energy defending your position.)

At larger companies, a few top women often become known as champions of other women. Eventually they become overwhelmed with requests, while the others around them are never asked to help. So consider reaching outside the inner circle. Maybe there's someone whose commitment to women's issues is overlooked because her boss is so famous for supporting women that no one ever notices her in the shadows.

You will make a mistake now and then. We all do. Years ago I met a woman who talked a good game about women and diversity. She was fun, ambitious, and smart. I fell for her talk and encouraged the company to hire her. Within six months it was clear she was a complete and total sellout. The further up the career ladder she went, the more she sucked up to the guys. Whenever she had the opportunity to grant someone a favor, she always gave it to the man she thought would advance her own career. Her department eventually was less female than when she came in—and previously it had been run by a man!

If you are new to your company and have yet to make many acquaintances, make a list of a half dozen women who you think are savvy, from the most senior executive to the smartest junior secretary. Ask each of them to lunch, one-on-one. You'll begin to form a relationship with at least some of these women. If they're not already part of a network (in which case they'll invite you to join), they may enjoy helping you create one.

Personally, the best informal network I ever belonged to was started by Julia Sprunt, the top woman at Turner Broadcasting.

One day, out of the blue, Julia called to say that she was talking to seven senior women in three different cities throughout the corporation. "The guys go away to golf or hunt or fish all the time," she said. "That's how they all got to know each other. We never do anything like that. So why don't we have a spa weekend?" All of us agreed.

My first eye-opener was that the company would pay for our weekend. The other women told me to treat the trip as a business expense, but I didn't see how I could justify billing the company for a massage and a facial. I was a good girl. If we were enjoying ourselves, could we also be working? I didn't know how to play the game yet. But I finally got up the nerve and asked my boss, who immediately approved it.

That first year we were gone a day and a half. Each of us was so uncomfortable stepping out of the box that we were afraid to stay away longer.

But we did it. We ate our meals together, we talked about the company, we had fun, and we all came away with a new understanding of our jobs. I learned more in those thirty-six hours than in any other comparable time period in my career.

The other benefit was subtle but real. Now that we knew each other, we added each other to our e-mail address books. When the head of marketing in New York sent out general memos to the executives, my name appeared on the list. It didn't really mean anything, but when the other executives saw my name, they now thought, "Here's another area Gail has entered." Each one of us found our power enhanced.

The next year our trip was longer, and the buzz about it around the company increased. Within an hour of returning, every one of our (male) bosses entered our offices wanting to know all about the weekend. The joke at the company was that we were plotting a palace coup.

In the end, the weekend enhanced our relationship with our bosses. They understood what we were doing, and admired it. They knew we had picked up a piece of the game that we hadn't known before.

But the real upshot: By pulling together, we were exerting more power than we had individually.

There are many ways to initiate teams in work situations. But whichever way you choose, it's important not to get distracted when you start, and to follow through once you've gotten it off the ground.

Note: Avoid using the phrase "let's get together" as just filler to take up space in a conversation.

Too often women meet another woman, hit it off, and say, "Let's get together for lunch." Ninety-five percent of the time you both go back to your office and neither of you ever makes that lunch happen, even though you both meant to.

So make it happen. That's how you continue to build the team.

It's time to mean what we say, and to take action on it. "Let's get together" means exactly that—a chance to solidify a connection. Get together.

Here's a good story: One day, before a meeting of oncologists in New Orleans, a sales representative from the drug company Aventis called a female oncologist and invited her to dinner. The oncologist said that she hated big fancy meals and would prefer having tea at the Windsor Court Hotel.

The two women, after having both an excellent tea and a great time, decided to ask some of the other oncologists to join them. So a year later, before the next meeting, the Aventis rep set up a tea for several women; this was such a worthwhile experience for everyone that the sales rep now decided to put together a "ma/spa" weekend for the doctors and their families where the women could get the latest medical updates and discuss their work and careers with their peers, all without having to leave their kids (or husbands) at home.

I find this kind of gathering very female. Rather than the fancy dinner or the golf game, these women opted for an informal barbecue that they could enjoy with their children. And it simply grew out of women talking to other women, and being authentic with each other.

• • •

Those female oncologists had no other option except to form a team with women outside their office—their own offices aren't large enough for teams.

For those of you who work at large organizations, even if

you are already in an internal organization, I urge you join another team, *outside your company*. For those of you who don't work at a large company, it's even more important— these teams are your best access to a supportive network.

Why spend even more of your time on business-related matters? First you thought your career was just about your work; then you were encouraged to join a team inside your office, and now I'm saying to network outside the office, too.

The answer: Making contacts gives you a safety net. Meeting with your peers provides you with information you can't learn inside your company. These groups tell you about jobs you might not otherwise ever hear about. They show you how other women are doing in your industry. They offer you friends in the industry outside your company, people whom you may want to employ or suggest for employment (or people who may suggest you). They provide you with a forum to talk about issues you can't, or don't want to, discuss at your office. They help you feel less alone.

Such alliances are easy to join. All you have to do is say that you're in the industry and sign up—in some organizations you don't even have to have an industry job (or a job at all), you can just be looking for work.

(As you move up the ranks, however, you will find more exclusive clubs where you may have to be nominated for admittance.)

Do a little research to find how it works in your industry. For example, if you're working in communications (or you want to), there are more than two dozen groups to consider joining, from the Association for Women in Communications to American Women in Radio and Television. In your town, one of those organizations will be the most powerful and have the most interesting people. This varies from city to city. If you are starting out new and fresh, pick the strongest of the groups.

These organizations exist for nearly every profession, but if for some reason your profession doesn't have one, here's a great opportunity to make a name for yourself: Start one.

A word of caution: You can spread yourself too thin. Never forget that your job is your primary focus. Don't belong to everything. Showing up at a different organization four nights a week won't help your career. Instead, find the group you think is good and get the most you can from it.

Alternative strategy: If you want to be a mover and shaker and you need a canvas to show off your ability, pick the organization that's not doing very well. You'll be able to make more of a difference in the weaker group.

No matter which group you join, attend meetings faithfully. Otherwise you'll defeat your purpose. Make it a regular obligation—the other women won't get to know you if you go once every nine months.

And if you don't like the organization? I once joined one of the top women's groups in the country only to discover that I clashed with the prevailing culture. It's the same as a job—don't enlist yourself anywhere you know you won't fit in. Check out the meetings first, and if you find the women boring, overly earnest, or anything else that turns you off, turn them off. Don't get too attached just because you heard that this organization was the best. Let go and join another. I did.

Power is constantly shifting back and forth in the corporate world, especially in this era of blockbuster mergers. One reason to have visibility in the community is that you have no idea whom you'll be working for in six months. But if you met a woman from another company when you worked on the multiple sclerosis society banquet, and suddenly she's your new boss, you'll have an advantage if she walks into the meeting, spots you across the room, and says, "Nice to see you, Susan."

If you use this advice strategically, it will help you—and all of us—to succeed. By giving women a leg up, we're just giving women the fair shot we deserve.

The single most important point: Just join.

PART 2

Tips for the Team

3
TEAM TIP ONE:
Be a Mentor

Mentoring isn't a discussion. It's an obligation.

Every female boss must study the women coming up the ladder and try to identify the potential stars. She must then help them achieve that stardom. Part of being on the women's team is taking care of other women. The higher up you go, the more women you take care of.

How else can we ensure that the younger women don't have to struggle with the same issues that the older women did? There's no value in having every woman make the same mistakes over and over, and then live through the consequences.

What exactly is mentoring? It means helping, any way you can. A mentor can teach; she can show by example; she can write books or lecture. She can also simply be a role model: If you are successful, women throughout your company and industry will watch you from a distance, often without your being aware of it. In other words, mentoring can be many different types of relationships, and like networking, it can be formal or informal; anything that works, works.

The formal mentor is the rare one-on-one connection with someone to coach them on how to play the game. Much of what you do is simply help people see where they truly want to go, and how they can get there.

Informal mentoring, which is relatively common, is not as structured as the formal mentoring relationship; it's more problem-specific. Here you help women who need precise advice at exact moments in their careers. I'm involved with a number of women in these more casual relationships. I talk to some of them several times a year, and others just once every few years.

Unfortunately, these days many women now believe they should have a different kind of mentor: a specific person who counsels them whenever they have a problem, someone whom they believe has an actual duty to help their career move along.

This kind of thinking can be dangerous. If you assume your mentor owes you something or has a specific obligation to you, mentoring becomes a chore rather than a relationship, and it stops becoming effective.

Many large companies now have formal programs in which a woman is assigned to a mentor who will supposedly make her life easier. That mentor is supposed to become the equivalent of a contact in the good old boy network—the guy down the hall's father's golf buddy or ex-college roommate.

The trouble is, as well-intentioned as these programs may be, they don't solve the real problem, which is that we're not mentoring each other often enough, nor are we doing it naturally. We have had to create this artificial system in its place. But no company-appointed mentor can take the place of a genuine mentor–"mentee" relationship. Both people have to be invested in working hard, and in caring.

The other day I gave a speech to the women of a division of one of America's largest companies. They'd asked me to talk about female mentoring, as they had recently instituted their first program. I asked them if the men had a similar plan. The answer was no—because the men had never asked for one. This made me realize that women have to be careful not to repeat the 1970s, when we wore those terrible, broad-shouldered dress-for-success suits and sported male briefcases as though we were trying to turn into men. By setting up these formal mentoring programs, we are taking something the men do naturally and formalizing it in an artificial way.

Question: Why don't the men need to learn about mentoring? Answer: They have instinctively mentored each other for generations. Every male boss loves finding the bright young man to succeed him. It's another feather in his cap—he's so smart, he's found a hotshot who can follow him up the ladder.

That's what women have to start doing too. We need to turn around and look. We need to find the women whom we like, whom we want to spend time with, whom we enjoy helping. When we do that, these formal mentoring programs will disappear.

Because we have to take baby steps before we fly, perhaps these programs, stiff and limited as they are, are those little strides. But truly good mentoring must arise from the fabric of our beings. Soon the time will come when mentoring is as natural to us as it is to the men. When this happens, we'll produce an entirely new, well-prepared generation of women ready to advance further than we ever could.

When you want to mentor:

Not every woman can be your formal mentee. In fact, very few can. The process only works well when there's a genuinely warm feeling between the two of you. I have met plenty of women who were smart and talented, but I just didn't like them enough, or have enough in common with them, or have the right chemistry, to be able to mentor them well.

When mentoring is forced, we don't achieve the real goal, which is to help other women achieve more, and more quickly, as naturally as possible.

A good mentor teaches, answers questions, and shows by example. Because she genuinely likes you, she has empathy for your situation, and understands the difficult choices that lie in front of you.

Throughout my career I have formally mentored no more than a dozen women. We met frequently and talked about everything from the large picture to fashion tips. One of the most important pieces of advice I've ever given was to a wonderfully talented young woman who wore white shoes to work in the fall. Even the normally fashion-challenged men recognized this as a mistake. It made her entire demeanor seem as though she weren't serious about her job; her self-presentation hadn't caught up with her ambition. When you're young and struggling to advance, you don't want to create distractions.

I felt uncomfortable making a comment, but I so wanted this woman to succeed that I called her into my office and, shaking, told her my thoughts. It worked. She was able to shift her perception of herself and of how others saw her, too. She stopped making silly sartorial errors, and she is now a highly successful executive.

Good mentors want their mentees to succeed because they see them as smarter and younger versions of themselves. I am proud White Shoes has had such a successful career. She has done us both proud.

These mentoring relationships are not totally selfless. I don't mentor people whom I don't want to be more powerful than me, or who may make changes I won't like. We mentor people who will make everything better for everyone, not just for themselves.

Mentoring is only a powerful force when it is natural and organic. Both of you must feel comfortable.

One final reason you mentor: You can't make your own success your only focus. If all you want is to get ahead, you don't bring others along with you, and you haven't formed relationships to help other women advance. Yes, some women *do* go it alone. But alone is always the hardest way to do anything.

Note: Mentoring comes in all shapes and sizes. For example, I know a small-business owner who says that one of her favorite ways to mentor is to let her staff watch how important it is to her to attend her son's hockey games. By doing so, her staff sees how a successful boss manages her time and sets her priorities. In fact, some of her male staffers have begun to identify with this mentoring and now show up for their own children's major events.

This kind of action also helps women create a more family-friendly workplace without sacrificing any business objectives.

When you want to be mentored:

Today it's easy to find mentors—many networking organizations offer programs, as do leadership groups within companies themselves. But as mentioned above, the most helpful mentors will probably be those you find yourself.

How do you find them? You listen, you look, you observe, you ask questions. You see a woman in your company whom you want to fashion yourself after, whom you can learn from, and you begin to ask her questions.

The word *mentor* itself gets in the way. Frankly, I feel weird when someone comes and says, "Will you be my mentor?" That feels unreal.

Instead try, "When you're free, will you have lunch with me? I'd like to talk to you about some confusing situations in my department." That's a real question and the beginning of a real relationship.

- *Start with a nice e-mail.* Tell your chosen candidate that you would like to take her out for a cup of tea or a drink, or come by her office and ask her how she became successful. Or, tell her you are thinking of making some changes in your career and ask for fifteen minutes to talk about it.

- *Make sure you have something to ask.* It's not your perspective mentor's job to make you feel comfortable. If you want advice, be ready to ask some intelligent questions, and know when to get up and leave.

- *Be smart about your mentoring relationship.* Many women have told me that the company has assigned them a mentor who asks her where she wants to be in her career in twenty years—and that's all the mentor seems interested in.

But what if you've had five different jobs in the last seven years, and you love the variety even though the moves are lateral? Your work has been interesting, challenging, and you don't want to get on a track. But your mentor insists you must.

To me, that isn't a mentor's responsibility. A mentor is someone who helps you figure out what you want and shows you how to get it. It's not someone telling you what you want and drawing you a procedural plan.

I know one woman, Marquita, who worked as a buyer in retail. Marquita had a proactive mentor who told her that, because she was so smart, she should go to business school and work her way up the business side of her company. Taking these words to heart, Marquita enrolled in graduate school and is currently a senior vice president at a major company.

The problem is that she would much rather be shopping than crunching numbers, which is all she does now. She's good at it, but she's miserable. The mentor gave sound advice for someone who wanted to climb the corporate ladder, but Marquita didn't. Following someone's advice doesn't make sense if the advice isn't right for you.

- **_Female mentors are generally preferable._** A female mentor can better help you maneuver through office morasses because she had to get through them herself. Most men don't even see the same difficulties women see. (Many of the men I know actually think they're the ones who have the problem— they feel they have to be so careful that they can't even breathe near a woman or she'll sue. These aren't the issues where you need help.)

One line of questions I constantly get from women concerns presentation issues: which lipstick, which dress, which earrings are appropriate. You probably wouldn't discuss such things with your male mentor, and even if you did, his answer might well be wrong.

Another line concerns balance issues: You are wondering about life and work as you consider pregnancy, and he's just not a good judge of how this will affect your career. He knows what he's supposed to say, but since he's never had to face the issue himself, he won't give you that special insider's insight.

And what about all those times when you feel the men are making you crazy and you want to talk about it? Tell that to a man and he won't get it, or at least, not the same way a woman does. (He won't even fully understand your use of the word *crazy*. Men don't think they're crazy. They just think that we are.)

Like it or not, many of your questions will have something to do with gender. Women always tell me that they don't know how to explain to their boss or male mentor that they're pregnant and want to slow down. He's a good guy, they say, and he gives lip service to my concerns, but he's still disappointed.

This happened to a woman who used to work for me. She had a great male mentor who saw her as a fast-tracker. Then she became pregnant with her second child. She came to me because she didn't know how to tell her mentor she truly cared about her career but that she wanted to go easy for a year. The mentor had been supportive through her first pregnancy, but she knew he thought all that was over and that now they could move ahead.

When she talked to me about these issues, she could say what she really thought. She couldn't do that with her mentor, which was why she needed female mentoring advice on how to deal with her male mentor.

Here's a story from an old workmate, Maya, who had met her husband on the job—they had been introduced at an office function, had fallen in love, and married. They had roughly equivalent careers at their company. Then the company changed hands and, during the restructuring, he was laid off while she wasn't.

This situation upset Maya terribly, and she soon approached her boss to say that she couldn't be part of this new team because of the way her husband had been treated. Maya's boss was disappointed but agreed to let her go.

While her severance documents were being prepared, Maya went to say good-bye to her mentor, Deborah. After listening to Maya's story, Deborah said, "I know what an excellent job you do and I know how much you love your work. Are you sure you want to do this? It's great that you're supporting your husband. But are you positive you're doing the right thing for *you*?"

Maya looked puzzled. "No one's asked me that," she said. "All I've thought about is what happened to my husband."

Deborah suggested Maya go home and think it over more carefully. She did, and the next day she told her friend, "You're right. I thought about how my children would feel if I stayed at a company that had fired their father. I thought about how my husband would feel if I came home and talked about my work at the company. But I never thought about how I felt. Last night I realized that I still love my job and want to stay."

After a few difficult conversations everything was straightened out and Maya remained in her job. Her husband, of course, landed a new position within weeks and never looked back.

• *Keep it natural.* Don't try to rearrange the entire bureaucracy of your company searching for women to help you. You may create trouble for yourself if you go over your boss's head to find a mentor. Understand your company's politics. Don't force a mentor relationship if it's out of whack with the company's policies.

- *Don't feel guilty.* As I said earlier, a lot of women feel their success doesn't count unless they make it on their own. But you get no more points for going solo than from getting a leg up. In this game, no one cares how many people helped you. What matters is where you end up.

- *Know that people may resent you.* Some people at CNN saw the handful of women I actively mentored being promoted, and there was plenty of resentment. There's little you can do about this, but it's a reality you must be aware of.

- *Mentoring can occur anywhere, anytime.* You don't need a job to be a mentor. My friend Shirley hasn't worked in many years, but she's so savvy and considerate that many women come to her for advice, including a mutual friend of ours named Alicia. Alicia always wanted a career in the art world, and not long ago she put together such a wonderful exhibit that several investors offered to back her in a gallery of her own.

This was Alicia's dream, but her confidence crumbled when it suddenly appeared possible. She knew she was creative, and she had excellent contacts in the art world, but she doubted her ability to run a business. Who would take care of the inventory, the accounts, even the janitorial services? The more she thought about it, the more doubts entered her mind—maybe she should let someone else own the gallery, and she could work for hire.

That's when Shirley rolled up her sleeves. She knew Alicia had great potential, so they met once a week for months as Shirley coached Alicia on how to be confident, how to take charge of her business, how to get done what needed to be done. Every time Alicia became frightened, Shirley would go over all of it again. Now, several years later, thanks to Shirley's mentoring, Alicia's gallery is a success, and Alicia can't believe that she once doubted her own ability.

One final note: *You are your own best mentor.* Know yourself and know what you need. Have the confidence to understand that most of the time you already know the right answer. Does it really take someone else to convince you to go sit down to talk to the boss about getting transferred to another division? Or can you mentor yourself into doing it?

Coach yourself into taking the actions to get what you want. No matter how many times your official mentor tells you to make a move, unless you are really ready to do it, nothing will happen.

How often are you in situations where you don't even have a clue? You want a new job in a new division, but you need four years of experience in the area, and you only have three. You think, "Maybe I don't have enough experience, but I can take courses or attend meetings where I can learn what I need to know, and that will be the equivalent of a year's worth of on-the-job training." This is self-mentoring.

This also means you must educate yourself proactively. Last weekend I attended a conference where women in their midcareers were talking about their businesses. Here was an opportunity to meet a hundred other successful women on an intimate level. These women were mentoring themselves, learning as much as they could on their own.

Whenever you read a good book about business, you are mentoring yourself. Listen to a tape, take a class, attend a lecture. Never forget that *you* are responsible for your career. Yes, take advantage of whatever help you can get, but if you enter a mentoring relationship thinking someone else will do it all for you, you'll become weaker rather than stronger. Don't wait for someone to open the doors for you. Open the doors yourself.

4 TEAM TIP TWO:
Rainmake

A female friend of mine, the general counsel of a large manufacturing company, believes, as I do, that women must work together. So when she needed a big-time specialist in labor law, she scoured her law-school directory for women who worked at the same law firm as the prominent male labor lawyer she wanted to hire. Sure enough, she found one. She called the classmate and explained that her company had a labor issue that needed resolution, and asked if the woman could set her up with the male labor specialist. Even though she didn't do the actual work, the female lawyer received the credit for bringing in the business.

A woman in charge of public relations at a big manufacturing firm needed to hire a meeting-planning outfit to put on a major global event. A friend of hers had been doing events like this for years as a volunteer for the United Way, and was just setting up her own business. The public relations woman took a chance and gave her friend the business, because she knew how good her friend was. The plan worked, and now the friend's firm is a leader in its field.

Unfortunately, the above instances are exceptions rather than the rule. While men do this kind of rainmaking all the time, women don't. Our instinct is simply to get the best person. The man's instinct is to get the person he wants to help.

Before you hire someone, do what I call a *change/shift*. It's as though you are working at your computer keyboard and you have to hit the shift key to call up the symbol you want. Here, you hit a change/shift key in your head. That key says, "Think of a woman when you are hiring."

You have to make a conscious decision to hit that shift button before you hire. Otherwise, you'll end up thinking later, "Why didn't I think of so-and-so before I recommended that guy from the tenth floor?"

If women don't do this, we open ourselves up to the charge I hear over and over from the men, which is that one of the major reasons women don't move ahead more easily is that we don't bring in enough business.

But the response I hear from women is, "That's *terrible*. You can't hire a woman just because she's a woman. It's more important to be fair."

But what is fairness, when it comes to hiring women? Is it fair that most women are at a disadvantage in business situations? Is it fair that our opportunities are fewer and that our pay is lower? After all, if we're not willing to hire women, who is? The men aren't going to do it. It's not their job.

In an ideal world, men and women would be equal and gender wouldn't matter. But the world isn't ideal. Traditionally, the person who is the best is usually the one who the guys say is the best. Women don't do homework to see if they're actually right. Maybe there are several women out there who are better, but no one really knows because people don't talk about them as much.

This is true from the lowest to the highest levels of work, whether you are looking to hire home cleaners or high-powered consultants. It's time for women to hire other women

Now, I'm not urging you to settle. Of course everyone wants to make sure they have the best lawyer, male or female. But the reality is, we haven't been doing our homework to find that best lawyer. Nor do we give women (and minorities) the chance to be the best at whatever they do.

Rainmaking is particularly important because, as a rule, the most important jobs usually go to the people who generate the most revenue for the company.

As mentioned, women lawyers work every bit as hard as their male counterparts but only constitute 12 percent of partners. Why? Because the lawyers who bring in the most business are the ones who are promoted.

It is true that in many businesses there is a distinction between the people who bring in the clients and the people who keep the clients happy. (This is especially true with personal services, like accounting.) These roles are often alleged to be equal. The truth is, they're not. The person who secures the business is higher up on the totem pole than the person who maintains the business.

Men believe it is harder to bring in the business than it is to keep it. Who knows whether they're right or wrong?

But one thing is certain: Without rainmaking, the company wouldn't survive, as it wouldn't have the cash flow—without that flow, the discussion can't even take place.

How does that revenue tend to flow? From your dad's golf partner's son to the fraternity brother who shares season tickets in the same stadium box as the CFO.

Traditionally women have been afraid to duplicate this setup—because of a fear that if a woman were to give her business to a female friend, she'd look like one of these militant feminists that the men (and many women) are always mocking. She worries the men will say, "We can't trust her to give the business to the best person. She just wants to give it to women."

(Note: We have to stop wondering what the men are thinking. When I spoke at that female oncologists' meeting, a major issue raised was: How do the male doctors feel about our having these meetings? I then asked, "Do you think that if this room was filled with men that they would wonder what the female doctors were feeling?" The obvious answer is that it never enters their minds. In fact, it's not even on their radar screens.)

Women want to be thought of as high-minded, upstanding, perfect. We're afraid of being accused of being overly strategic or self-serving.

We don't get that being strategic or self-serving is what business is about. You do everything you can to help your company and yourself.

So we make up all these reasons to appear high-minded and not as though we're simply doing a favor for a friend. But there's a good reason to do a favor for a friend: You can trust friends.

• • •

Rainmaking is the only way we can begin to improve our increasingly depressing numbers. After all, if every woman in America decided to find a female lawyer, the percentage of female partners would jump from 12 to 50 very fast.

If you are in a position to hire, you are in a position to make a difference.

Let's say you work at a small not-for-profit organization and you're looking for an accountant. Do you see an opportunity to hire a woman? Or do you go with that male accountant everyone knows? When you're the general counsel, do you give the outside work to another woman? Or do you go with the same people who have been working with the firm for the last thirty years?

If you want to start slowly, begin at home. When you're giving a party or a shower, you'll spend a certain amount of money. Stop to think if there's a female photographer, or a female caterer, or a female florist as good as the male service-providers your friends use. After you become habituated to thinking about hiring women in your private life, transfer that habit to your job.

Besides helping to increase women's visibility, rainmaking has many advantages. As women make more money and have more responsibility, they become more powerful. That makes you more powerful, too. (Remember, we're only as strong as the weakest member of the team.) Whenever a woman gets the business, it helps you, it helps me, it helps us all.

Rainmaking breaks down barriers. You never know when your suggestion to hire the female job seeker will not only be accepted, but will mean the first woman has that position at your company.

The more women rainmakers, the more the stereotype of women as the business servicer and the men as business finder gets broken down. Many men believe women are afraid to ask for business and therefore can never be as powerful as men. It's not true, but there's only way to prove it. Do it.

Hiring women can improve your image at the office. In today's business climate you accumulate points for helping the company solve its diversity problems. Bringing in excellent women will make you shine in a world where no company wants a staff composed only of white males. Also, once you are known for giving women a chance, you will find that the very best women hear of you and seek you out.

It's the rainmakers who usually rise to the top of the company (and their professions). It's not uncommon for the head of sales to become chairman, but that's almost impossible for the head of human resources. The more women rainmake, the more likely we are to obtain all the great perks of being at the top, which include the ability to hire more women as assistants, drivers, travel agents, and so on.

And, by learning to rainmake, we will show everyone, including ourselves, that we are not afraid to take chances, because anytime you deal with areas outside your expertise, such as revenue or marketing, a risk arises. The perception that women are overly cautious is another reason we are held back from those top jobs.

But there's still one more reason to rainmake. Your female accountant may understand and handle your problems better precisely because she's a woman. You may find you can ask her intimate questions you couldn't or wouldn't ask a guy. Sometimes, as much as you may not want to admit it, because it doesn't seem fair, a woman fits the bill better than a man.

• • •

To become a good rainmaker, here's what you must do:

• *Make sure you always think about women when the subject of jobs comes up.* If part of your job is determining who gets the business, don't forget to ask yourself: "Is there a woman in my circle I should consider here?"

In the beginning, because the names of appropriate women may not automatically pop up, you may have to do a little research or you may have to ask several people in your network. Use your imagination. There are more resources than you think. For example, the other day my neighbor was complaining that she wanted to hire a capable woman to redo her house, but she couldn't find one. I told her all she had to do was go to the newsstand, where she would find a local magazine called *Atlanta Woman* with a section listing women-owned businesses in every issue.

If you're the person in human resources who does the hiring for the typical male jobs, make an extra effort to think about women. Companies that were once male-run only have changed. For instance, janitorial services: Many of these firms are now female-run.

Thirty years ago my friend (and single mother) Judy Hanenkrat decided that what she knew best in life was how to clean a house. With only a hundred dollars and some cleaning equipment, she began a residential cleaning service, passing out fliers, ringing doorbells, and meeting with apartment managers to drum up business. Soon Judy's business had grown large enough that she could hire a staff, and eventually she switched to cleaning office buildings. Now she has a large company. Do you think about offering women like Judy a job?

Another woman I know was a struggling sales rep for a firm that manufactures mugs emblazoned with company logos. Her friend, a TV producer, had a show that decided to give out mugs to the viewers who wrote the best letters to the on-air host. The producer gave her friend the business of making those logo mugs, and she did such a good job that the network's other shows soon followed suit. My young friend became one of her company's top salespeople.

• **Don't hide.** Rather than downplay your assets so that you can look like the nice girl your mother told you to be, make sure that people know how skilled and talented you are.

The time for covert behavior has passed. I don't think any of us should be allowed to get away with the shy smiles and behind-the-scenes movements that characterized women several generations ago. You're not a full team player if you're covert. And the team is not playing smart if we don't pass along the best information we have about everyone—including ourselves.

- **Be proud of your title.** Too often women don't pay attention to other women's titles. We think the guys are silly to care about such trivial matters; we know it's not about the trimmings, it's about the substance. (Still, we always get the guy's titles correct, because we know they'll be upset if we don't.) Vice president, senior vice president, executive vice president, is there really a difference?

Yes. Trimmings are part of the workplace. If you spent years fighting for a new title, wear it proudly. It's about how powerful you are. Make sure others know.

Most people want to send their business to a firm or an individual who has a first-rate reputation, who is considered outstanding in her field. If you don't present yourself as such, you're not as likely to get the assignment. When you talk about your friend the accountant and you say how nice and smart she is, that's fine. But you also need to say that she services the BellSouth account or that she won the award as her firm's top accountant of the year, or any other important fact.

When I tell women to do this, they think I'm telling them to boast, and they become uncomfortable. But if I say, "Just be your own best public relations person," they get it.

Not long ago I spoke at a women's group where the moderator asked those present to stand and introduce themselves. They did, and you would never have known that these were some of the most prominent women in corporate America. At least two thirds of the room were simply incapable of saying who they were. They uttered statements such as, "I work in sales," or "I'm at the Such-and-Such company," failing to mention that they were the CFO, or the senior vice president, or the head of marketing. Perhaps these women thought their modesty was attractive, but I found it irritating and a hindrance to the discussion at hand. How can we stride forward if we're all pretending that our achievements don't matter?

- *Develop a quick résumé.* To make sure that other women can rainmake for you easily and efficiently, develop a succinct, one paragraph description of yourself. Memorize a couple of sentences that are clever and smart, so if you're stuck, you can shift into your rote speech. Too often we're asked to explain our position, and we hem and haw and then an hour later think, "Now I know what I should have said!"

Practice saying it aloud to make sure that you're comfortable. You don't want to run halfway through it, turn bright red, and excuse yourself from the room.

- *Watch the good rainmakers.* Look at the men and women who do it well. Don't be shy about asking them questions. Why did they recommend that person? What are they going to do next?

- *Be visible.* Don't just join the organization—become known for something. Run for president. Run the newsletter. The more people who know about you, the more likely they are to rainmake for you—and the more likely you are to meet other women whom you may be able to help someday.

- *Good rainmaking comes out of good networking.* When I give a speech and a woman in the audience enjoys it, she's likely to recommend that her organization hire me. Everyone I speak to is a potential rainmaker for me. They move me from one speech to the next.

The advantage for my rainmaker: If I do a good job, she gets listened to again, and may get authority to act more independently the next time. (Just as if I do a bad job, it will reflect badly on her.)

Just the other day a woman whose company hired me on her recommendation told me that, because everyone liked my speech, it made her look better. "People think I have more clout than I really do," she said, "because I had a very visible success."

- *If you help give a woman a job, continue your support.* Yes, it's great that you went out of your way to hire that woman to be your number two. Don't abandon her now. I just heard the story of a recently promoted CEO of a Texas-based company who hired another woman to take her old job as CFO. But once the young woman arrived, the CEO basically continued to do both her new job and her old one, constantly undermining the young woman.

Always remember that when you bring in another woman, part of your job is to help her prosper. What's the point of hiring a woman if you stop her from succeeding?

• • •

I am not saying that you must always hire a woman. It shouldn't (and can't) be done. And not everyone I've hired is a woman. For example, my financial planner is male. I do feel some guilt about this and wonder if I should find a female replacement. But I don't, because there's another way to guarantee that women get the jobs, even when you've already hired a male. I make sure that I talk about these issues to my planner so that he is aware of how I feel. Knowing I'm about to refinance my house, my planner said, "I have the name of a great mortgage banker who can get it done for you. It's a woman," he added, "because I wouldn't offer you a man." In a way he was kidding, but he also wasn't.

Yes, we all want the best. I'm not saying you shouldn't. I'm asking, "Did you stop and see if there was a woman who was the best, or did you even consider a woman? Or did you do what everyone else does and simply go with the man?"

And if you do decide to work with a man, are you going to make sure that he knows how you feel, so that when it comes time to hire someone else, he will look as hard for a woman as a man?

Today, when a company engages in a search to find a new CFO, it may come up with a list containing six people. And if we're lucky, there may be one woman on that list. We need to make sure this list is half female, just like half the work force. And these should be women with whom the power structure is familiar, not simply people who are on the list because someone felt it was politically correct.

We will only be considered for the real positions when we have real power based on real experience.

5

TEAM TIP THREE:
Uncover and Share
Information

Last week my friend Kate told me about a meeting that had taken place at her company. It was the Monday morning strategy conference, and she was very proud of the fact that, as the new marketing director, the Top Guys had asked her to attend.

I then asked her how the system worked. She explained that the five men held the meeting each week, and that the key person in each of six departments, including marketing, sales, and human resources, presented an informal report.

Further questioning led me to ask how many of these six were women. "Four," Kate said proudly.

"How well do you know these other women?" I asked.

"Pretty well," she said. "We go out to lunch frequently, and we get along. In fact, the men are always congratulating us on our camaraderie."

"That's great," I said. "Now, how much do you know about their departments?"

"Very little," she replied. "I'm not in their departments. Why would I know about them?"

And therein lies the problem. The men are taking in a complete overview of the entire business, while the women remain experts only in their individual areas.

One of the reasons men use to explain our failure to advance: We don't have a complete picture.

In part, this is true because we aren't offered the jobs that give us this overview. But women could get around that problem if we would only share our business lives with each other. We don't. At lunch we're willing to talk about the most intimate details of our daily existence, sex with our husbands, our kids' school problems. Business is the one thing we don't talk about enough—unless it's to complain about people we don't like or tasks we have to complete. Too often we act as though business were a taboo subject.

This turns us into isolated experts. We're not familiar with the big picture. I hear this over and over when a woman isn't promoted. The men say, "She was great, but she didn't have the sales experience," or the marketing experience, or whatever area it is we don't know that they throw at us.

A recent study from Catalyst showed that 82 percent of the male CEOs interviewed—82 percent!—said that the major justification for not promoting women is their lack of significant experience outside their own area of expertise.

What can we do about it?

Kate's situation is not unusual. In most companies a handful of men constitutes the basic power structure. And when they hold their meetings, they'll often invite one woman—

the expert in marketing, or human resources, or finance. She then spends that one day in the inner circle. The next time, the invitee is the woman who knows brand development or the woman who knows the numbers.

Women tend to work in isolation. This is partly because we are often very uncomfortable about whether or not to trust someone. We're always saying to colleagues, "Don't tell anyone else." And when a woman hears another woman repeat something she was told privately, she feels it's a breach of confidence. "She shouldn't have told me that," she thinks.

The men think only the Really Big Stuff is confidential. Women think everything is. That means that we have a tendency to hoard information. And when we do share, we do it in stingy ways. We never sit around together and talk openly. We share information quietly, behind closed doors.

Candace walks into her best friend's office and says, "Let me tell you what just happened." She then says the same thing to four other women, and all are sworn to secrecy. Each then may tell another friend, and the news is spread like the old game of telephone—which also means that each time the information is passed along, it becomes less accurate.

What are you missing when you don't share what you know? A great deal of information that might otherwise be unavailable to you. Is this a company where there's a meeting before the meeting? Or is the official meeting all there is? Who sits at the table, and why? What do people wear, who is trustworthy, how can you make the boss look good? You learn how to fit in the big picture, instead of trying to make the picture fit you.

The more information you have, the better your job performance. One reason the Big Bosses are big is because they know more than you do.

And as you become more comfortable sharing information, the job becomes easier. Many women, when assigned a task, think they have to know everything about the particular subject at hand, becoming a quasi expert in whatever must be known, instead of just picking up the phone and asking a friend for help. We feel like an impostor if we get the information from someone else. Shouldn't we have to do all the work ourselves? Isn't that what we were taught?

Perhaps, but it's time to change. Here's how:

- *Start an information exchange.* Just as you look around for other women to create teams, look around for women with expertise in the areas of the company you should know something about. These are women with whom you feel a natural fit, whom you would enjoy talking to. As with every other rule, if you apply force, it won't work. It must feel natural. But it's hard to believe that you can't find at least a few women in your company to initiate the conversation.

- *Talk about work.* When you go out to lunch with your female colleagues, change the subject. You can always talk about the baby-sitters and the dry cleaners, but don't forget to talk about the job. Formalize these conversations, just as you have formalized teams. Create small groups of women to discuss the business from varying perspectives.

A side benefit: When you have information that seems to have come from someone a level above, the power structure feeds you even more information. Last month I heard a story about a Southwestern manufacturing company where the executive women noticed that, like Kate above, they were always being invited to small high-level corporate meetings one at a time. So after every meeting, these women began to assemble and share what that one invitee had just learned.

This knowledge not only made them more aware of current developments, its unexpected result was that the men told them even more. Why? Once a woman could show the men through her casual conversations that she knew the problems they were dealing with, the assumption in the good old boy network was that she had an in with one of them. As a result, they viewed her as more powerful.

• *Forget the idea that personal and business conversation are completely separate.* We'll talk more about this in Chapter 9, but understand that there is no such thing today as completely separate personal and business lives. This is not a bad thing. It gives us the opportunity to bring our best skills from our personal lives to the office. It gives us the chance to make relationships wherever we go, and in some cases, make deeper ones, because they have significance in both spheres. By letting your professional and personal lives flow together, you'll find more opportunities for growth in both.

• *Ask questions.* Create a context where you're comfortable asking whatever you need to know. We often feel uneasy asking another woman a lot of questions. When a woman hears a story, she listens, she may ask a question or two, but for the most part, she thinks it's rude to ask too much. When a man hears the same story, he'll ask as many questions as he feels are necessary for him to understand.

This doesn't mean that you should take up everyone's time in the big meeting asking dozens of questions. It means using your colleagues as an informal resource. If you are working on a project that has marketing implications, you don't have to spend your time becoming a marketing expert. Learn to pick the brain of the smartest people in marketing. In the quest for perfection, women think they have to learn it all from the beginning. What they have to learn is who to ask.

• **_Don't expect complete confidentiality._** I always used to tell my staff not to bother locking information in their computers. "If you do," I would say, "you start to believe that life can be confidential."

Today, in this open information-minded society, nothing is truly confidential. Your bosses can probably find out anything they want, no matter how many locks you've put on it. It is always best to operate as though you are an open book. Anyway, you don't get caught in as many mistakes when you operate publicly. I learned that from living in Moscow, where my husband was transferred in the 1960s. There our apartment and our car were bugged, and we knew it, and they knew we knew it. It didn't really affect our life, but it was an excellent lesson in understanding that there's very little you ever need to hide.

• **_Get over the idea that other women are competitors._** Women often hoard information from other women because they see them as direct competitors. But today, everyone is a competitor, male or female. If you single out women to compete against, you only make it easier for the men.

• ***Don't expect more than information.*** Let's say that you have to launch a project that needs sales support, so you ask your friend in the sales department to lunch so you can talk to her about your new task. That sales person's job isn't to make your life easier. She isn't going to give you information that might hurt her department for a friend's sake. She has to protect her staff. But she will provide you with ideas on how to make your project work from a sales point of view, and she can also be your sales ally when you are ready to present.

Furthermore, if you have a victory, and the boss thinks you did a good job presenting that project, your friend in sales has a victory, too.

• ***Information doesn't have to come from direct contact.*** Did you read your company's latest annual report? When I asked this question at a recent speech for Fortune 500 female mid-level executives, most of the women said they hadn't. That's a mistake. Annual reports contain invaluable information about your company that you should know.

Likewise, do you read the clippings about your company when it's covered in the media? If you do, you're gathering information for the whole team. Years ago one of my secrets to success was entering early morning meetings already having read all the necessary newspapers. This meant I had information no one else had. I would now say that if I were truly on the team, I would have e-mailed another woman whom I respected the same information, so that both of us could look good.

This may not come naturally at first, because being the only one in the know feels great. But we've reached a point where being a team player has definite advantages. Remember that the team will find a way to help you back.

Note: If your boss always gets his or her information from easily available sources such as the *New York Times* or *Business-Week*, make sure you always read them before you see him or her.

- **Share information whenever it can help.** But use common sense about whom to trust and how much to tell. Don't tell someone with a big mouth about upcoming, secret layoffs in her department, or pass along negative news to someone who tends to overreact. But if you have a piece of knowledge that an ally could use, find a smart way to let her know.

You don't always have to be direct. If you know someone's budget is going to be cut, you don't have to tell her in so many words. Find a clever way to pass along your information. You could say, "I'm getting bad vibes about money at this company," in order to help her focus on the future. Or, you could start a general conversation about budgets. Think before you speak.

When the economy started going sour in the early 2000s, I was asked to discuss career strategy at a meeting with the top female players at an investment banking company. The woman who had invited me believed that the people who go first in tough economic times are the ones who bring in the least money. In this corporation, many of the top-level women were not generating the same kind of revenue as the guys—these women were more likely to be maintaining the business rather than doing the rainmaking. So she wanted to bring the women together to teach them strategies so that the upcoming layoffs wouldn't affect them any more than the men.

This woman was an ultimate team player. She not only shared all the information she could, but she created a forum so all the women she knew could share, too.

- *Always be listening with a strategic mind.* Important information isn't heard just in the boardroom. You can pick it up in the ladies' room, at the table next to you in the restaurant, or by the copy machine. Regard everything you hear as potential information rather than ambient noise.

As a member of the television industry, I got some of my best ideas for talk shows by listening to conversations at the dry cleaner, the bank, and the gym. I learned what people outside my professional circles were talking about. And I knew I was off-base when the conversations I was hearing weren't the same ones I was having.

- *Talk on planes.* Many women refuse to talk to anyone when they're flying. I'm guilty of this, too. When I'm sitting in an airplane, I like total silence. It's one of the few places I know I can work without being disturbed.

But I also know that a plane is a fabulous business vehicle. You could ride around in first class all your life and do nothing but drum up business, or gather information. Today, if the person next to me wants to talk, I force myself to enter the conversation and learn about his or her business. The result is that, over the last few years, I've sat next to some of the world's most fascinating people whose conversations have made me smarter.

- *When you share confidences, you find out you're not crazy.* There have been many times when work made me question my sanity until, through conversations with other women, I discovered they were going through the same convolutions. The more you talk to other women, the more you realize that your problems are not unique. The more you share, the more perspective you will have about your situation.

Take the case of Ashley, who works at a company where there are many female employees, but only a handful who have any power. When the Big Boss calls his planning meetings, he routinely invites the same six top male executives, and then invites Ashley or one of the other two women at her level—although seldom at the same time.

Ashley has an excellent relationship with the boss, who highly values her thoughts and respects her work. She knows this for a fact. Apart from the other meetings, they meet once a week to go over her department, and these one-on-one conferences are always helpful. But at the big meetings, Ashley has noticed that the men can blither on and on and never seem to say anything substantive, but the boss listens patiently, nods, and lets the speaker finish his thoughts. But whenever Ashley speaks, the boss cuts her off before she makes her point.

This pattern has troubled her enormously. Yet she didn't

feel she could say anything to the men about it, because she feared it would make her look diminished, and perhaps even paranoid. The more she thought about it, the crazier she felt. Maybe the boss wasn't cutting her off. Maybe she had said everything he wanted to hear, and she just didn't know it. Or maybe the men had a special way of getting his attention in large meetings, and if she were smarter, she could figure it out. Her head started spinning with all the possibilities for what might be happening, or what could be happening, or what didn't happen. For the first time in her life, Ashley, an otherwise completely rational woman, began to wonder if she was sane.

In the meantime, Ashley decided she should make some female friends in the company. The other women at her level were her competitors, but they all basically liked each other and decided they had nothing to lose by forming an association. Starting with a monthly lunch, they slowly forced themselves to share confidences about work, trusting the other women to be allies, not enemies.

Finally Ashley confessed her feelings about these meetings and how crazy the boss was making her. She was somewhat startled when the other women laughed. "Don't you know?" one of them said. "He always cuts off women at those meetings. It happens to every one of us."

She went on to explain that in these kinds of situations, the boss treats women the same way he treats his wife in public: He interrupts her, and then he talks over her. It may not be polite, but it's not really disrespect. The man knows that he will eventually hear whatever his wife wants to say in another venue, even if it's in bed.

"Don't you always have satisfactory private meetings?" one of the women asked. Ashley nodded. She, too, had seen the boss interrupt his wife this way, but she had never put it together with his behavior at the office. Ashley wasn't crazy. It turned out that all the women had to deal with this idiosyncrasy. Now that she knew, she felt sane again.

• • •

No one person has all the information. But if you hoard whatever knowledge you have, you are keeping the team from advancing. When you share this information, you make the team more powerful. Share the information, share the power.

6 TEAM TIP FOUR:
Keep Quiet

Here's a story that I know very well: A woman I'll call Hillary was working on an important female-oriented project which, if it had gone forward, would have changed her career. However, it didn't work out, and the reasons her male bosses gave her for shelving it were fair and probably accurate. Hillary moved on to other agendas, and her career flourished.

About five years later, Beth, another woman at Hillary's company, decided to propose that same idea, with a somewhat different approach. Before she made her move, Beth briefed Hillary on her plans, explaining why she thought that this time the men at the top might be more receptive. Hillary told Beth that she genuinely wished her well.

Indeed, Beth made more headway with the project than Hillary had, as the five intervening years had created a different stage—the economic atmosphere was better and the idea seemed more relevant.

Then one day, out of the blue, one of the Big Bosses took Hillary aside and essentially said in so many words: "Beth stole your idea and she's getting all of the credit."

Hillary was now feeling more than a little jealous. Her idea was moving ahead without her. She was also having second thoughts. Had she made a mistake in dropping the idea? Should she have told Beth that she wanted to team up with her? Was she playing this poorly from a political viewpoint?

Hillary said to her boss, "Yes, she did take my idea." Hillary and the boss then proceeded to talk about how Beth should have given Hillary more credit.

Afterward Hillary felt reassured. Her boss had taken her into his confidence and told her his concerns about the other woman. He seemed to trust her more than he did Beth. She felt she and he had bonded in a new way. Hillary felt guilty for dumping on her colleague, but she felt angry, too, and was glad to have had a chance to express that anger.

As far as Hillary was concerned, once she had vented, the story was over. But the boss had different point of view. From that moment on, every time a potential gender issue arose, he would look at her and say, "Hillary knows exactly what I mean."

As hard as Hillary tried, she was never able to convince the boss that despite that one incident, she liked and supported Beth, and that all she had been voicing in his office that day was her momentary irritation that Beth hadn't spent more time asking for her advice. And she never stopped helping Beth, who is still working on the project. Yet for the rest of Hillary's career, the boss used their conversation as proof that women can't get along.

The lesson Hillary learned: When a woman talks about

another woman to a man, it holds more water than when one of the guys makes a similar comment. Unless you're lucky, that comment can and will be used against you for life. Guys remember what women say about each other. You may think it's an idle comment, or a simple piece of information you are supplying in a business context. I say it is ten times bigger than that. You need to be prepared in each of those moments for the information you give to be used powerfully.

• • •

Now that I've told you to share information, I'm telling you to be quiet—because different situations have different rules. (Keep in mind that all rules must be flexible, and that you will get into trouble if you try to follow them literally. They only work when they apply naturally to your situation. You can't force a rule to apply any more than you can force a romance to blossom.)

When it comes to business information, share as much as possible, but keep your mouth shut when you are talking to men about other women. I don't care if this sounds tough and narrow-minded. It's absolutely essential.

Now I know a lot of you will fight me on this. You will give me a million and one reasons why I'm wrong. You will talk about your integrity and why being on the team shouldn't mean giving up your standards, and how you could never support someone—of either sex—who wasn't good.

Even if you violently disagree with me, I request that you keep an open mind and listen.

Over and over I've seen women sabotage careers by unintentionally putting other women down. I've observed this everywhere I've worked, and I've heard about it at practically every company where I've spoken.

In a business context, when a woman talks about another woman, she gives validity and power to any negatives that have been spoken about that woman. She also continues to perpetuate all the unfortunate stereotypes about women.

And when you do harm to another woman, you ultimately end up harming yourself, because in the great big world of business, women are seen as a group. That's the point of this book. When the woman down the hall gets promoted, that's good for you. And when the woman down the hall is fired, that's bad for you.

Think of Jill Barad, the former CEO of Mattel, who was fired after the toy company's stock plummeted. She has become the excuse for anyone and everyone who thinks a woman shouldn't be CEO. As far as the media is concerned, as well as corporate America, her name now signifies that a woman failed. This is particularly bizarre because she didn't fail at Mattel. She failed as the CEO at Mattel—but she is responsible for a huge percentage of the innovation of the Barbie system. There she performed brilliantly. If she hadn't been so good, how would she have managed to become CEO? Yet all the talk is about how a woman couldn't do the top job. And as long as that particular perception continues, every one of us will have to prove ourselves a little more.

Guys fail as CEOs all the time. Usually, they just end up as CEO someplace else.

If you believe you are different, if you think the men you work with only see you for the quality of your work, I say that you're wrong. You are not different; you are naive. Yes, the men see you for the quality of your work. But they never forget you are a woman.

Let's say you're having a problem with your new female boss, Allison, and one of the Big Guys takes you aside, looks at you soulfully, and whispers, "I just don't feel good about Allison's performance. I don't think her promotion is working out." In the meantime, you're struggling to get ahead and here's a Big Guy telling you something in confidence. And maybe you, too, have questions about Allison.

The average woman, thinking of her integrity, might say that Allison is very nice but then share all her problems with the boss. She believes that by doing so, she is being constructive. She's not playing politics because she thinks all the boss wants is her opinion.

I say: If you want to help yourself and the other women on the team, you tell the Big Guy that what he's saying is interesting, but that you personally weren't aware of it, and that now you'll be on the lookout. And add, because you are a team player, if there is any way you can support Allison, you certainly will.

A lightbulb has now been lit for you, and it's shining on something you hadn't seen before: They are gunning for Allison. And even though you dream that if Allison's gone, you will advance, you must remember that if they use you to get rid of Allison, they will use one of your employees to get rid of you.

So now you find a reason to mosey down the hall and help Allison do a better job.

Many of you may still object, and say, "I'm a team player, but I play for the Big Team. I'm not just in it for the women.

I have to tell the truth. I am not going to support some woman who's bad at what she does."

I say: Stop, breathe, and think before you talk about another woman. The chances are your words can ultimately affect not just her, but you and all the other women too.

Worse, you can't erase it once you've said it. It won't go away. It hangs over both of you forever.

I realize that many of you are still unsure about this. Whenever I give a speech, I know nearly all of the points I make are well accepted, because I see the audience nodding or smiling. When I give them this rule, I watch them go stone cold. They are thinking, "No! I won't do that."

This is not an assault on your integrity. I am not recommending you lie or deceive. I'm saying you shouldn't enter a dialogue about a female colleague. You simply may have no comprehension of the power you are bringing to the discussion. No matter that you intend your remarks to be casual or off-the-cuff, they can mortally wound a member of your team.

What do you do if another woman is spreading bad news about you? Get with the program and understand the consequences of talking about each other. Instead of concentrating on it, ask yourself if a fight would undermine your career. There are huge consequences to these battles. Know that ahead of time.

And, make sure that she's really dumping on you. Sometimes we imagine we're being attacked when she's just trying to sound smart or impress a boss—in other words, she was only thinking of her career. She doesn't care about yours.

Of course, if you're hearing her gossip through the boys,

make sure they're not exaggerating her words. Maybe they're just having fun. Some boys love a catfight. Don't indulge them.

Still, your best response depends on the situation. You can choose to ignore the woman, to laugh it all off, or to handle it yourself. Never go to the powers above you. Instead, approach the woman and make sure she knows that you get it, and tell her to pick on someone else. You'd be surprised how often the direct approach works.

Note: Too often women allow men to divide and conquer us. When they take us into their confidence, when they allow us the chance to speak privately about another woman, we succumb; we are so flattered that they are talking to us that we talk too much. Later, if they or we get into trouble, we defend ourselves by saying, "but he confided in me," giving the impression that confidences from a man are more meaningful than those from a woman.

7

TEAM TIP FIVE:
Unite with All Women
at All Times

Writer Gloria Steinem tells the story of a Northeastern university where women were not being tenured at the same rate as their male counterparts. In fact, over the last decade, the rate of promotion of women to the rank of full professor hadn't increased an iota.

The women were angry and frustrated. They wrote letter after letter; they appeared before committee after committee; they formed task force after task force. Nothing worked. They even tried a brief strike, but the men shrugged it off.

One day one of the female professors was describing her exasperation to her secretary, who sympathized deeply. As they talked, an idea hatched. Not many weeks later, all the secretaries went on strike in support of the professors.

Within a short time the male power structure caved, and the promise of more tenured jobs for female professors was a reality. The truth is that the female professors' refusal to show up for classes had no real effect on the male professors, but the assistants' refusal to show up for work, to answer the phones, and to take care of the mail did.

• • •

Because everything you do affects other women, playing on the women's team doesn't mean playing just with the women at your level. Nearly all women experience the same work-related problems, whether they're the only women in the mail room or the only women on the executive floor. Try to meet with the secretaries, with the senior vice presidents, and with everyone in between, because the front needs to form on all levels.

At CNN, I used to give the cleaning women books if they were trying to pass a high school equivalency exam, or offer advice to the security guards if they wanted to work in sales. I did this because I liked them—and because I saw that their success was connected to my success. Perhaps by making it clear that we all work together, women you might ordinarily overlook will become your greatest allies. We all pay each other back in different ways. These women may not improve your position at the office. But who knows? One of them may succeed at a level you don't dream of. You have no idea what the possibilities are for them, or how they can change the way their group of women looks at other women.

Too often, focused on getting ahead, we only think about the women who are above us. Can the senior woman in your company, or your boss, or that new executive vice president, help you?

Furthermore we feel that if we're seen with people more

important than we are, we'll look more important. Being seen with women below us, however, will reflect badly on us. Do we look good enough? we keep asking. Are we associated with the right people? Are we connected to the real power? We turn up our noses at those who aren't at our level.

We have to develop the self-assurance to understand this is wrong. Not everyone has the same ambition; not everyone wants to become CEO. Plenty of women achieve success on the lower rungs of the corporate ladder and decide that's where they want to stay, becoming experts at their job and the corporate culture. Respect them for the decisions they have made.

Some of the most knowledgeable and powerful women in any company are the assistants, the secretaries, and the associates. Think of the executive assistant—she's almost as important as the executive. Certainly she's almost as important to you and to the company. I just heard about a Fortune 500 CEO who was relocating to a new city, and all he could talk about amid his company's restructuring was how he could get his assistant to move with him; he didn't feel he could do his job as well without her.

These women have a store of knowledge about the company that isn't accessible to you. Over the course of my career assistants have clued me in dozens of times about what to steer clear of: not to make an appointment with the Big Guy on a specific day, not to ask a specific question or mention a specific person. At the same time they suggested it would be a good idea to bring up certain problems and issues. There were many moments when I might have made a complete fool of myself if a thoughtful assistant hadn't guided me in the right direction.

These women can be the gateways to power, and if you're not nice to them, they may hurt you. If you don't believe me, try setting up a meeting with a boss whose assistant doesn't like you.

(And yet who is always treating these women the worst? Other women—because of our own insecurities. Meanwhile, the guys, no fools, are sending these women flowers and remembering their children's birthdays.)

I'm not just talking about executive secretaries. I know a book editor whose contracts always seem to be completed faster than anyone else's because the woman who runs the contracts department is her friend. This means the editor's primary contacts—the book agents—trust her to get things done more quickly than other editors. That's a big bonus. I know a lawyer whose firm relies heavily on paralegals for all kinds of tasks; this woman has made sure that this staff (which is composed mostly of women) likes working for her more than any other lawyer. The result? Her work is finished first. Most importantly, as you begin to have genuine relationships with all women, you make the team more powerful. It's no longer just a bunch of ambitious women heading for the top. Now, it has depth.

• • •

The first step to take:

• *Stop being a snob.* You are not the one and only. Many women think they give more, do more, care more, feel more, and know more than anyone else. They often refuse to unite with other women because they feel no one is as committed as they are. Because these women also believe that promotions are based simply on performance and hard work, they see no advantage to being with others who don't give as much as they do.

Fact: Getting ahead is not just about who can do the actual work. A lot of people can. It is a matter of many nuances. These include everything from your connections, your appearance, and your brains to your ability to get along with the other women in your company, at all levels. Never underestimate the power of teamwork. And that means never underestimating the power of being able to include everyone you want on your team, whether she has an advanced degree or is trying to get her high school equivalency diploma.

- *Act natural.* You will like some of the women in your office and you won't like others. That's life; let it breathe. Maybe an assistant reminds you of your favorite Aunt Matilda. Do you chat to her and find out how similar the two women are, or do you talk down to her?

    You can't pretend everyone is your best friend and ask them all to lunch. Just don't close down the possibility that any one of these people could be your ally and even help your career—as well as vice versa.

- *Request information.* As discussed, be ready to ask questions. When you're outside the boss's office waiting for a meeting, instead of sitting silently or reading an old magazine, stand up, walk over to the assistant, and start talking. A conversation that begins as pleasant banter can develop into one that's filled with information.

- *Make friends throughout the family.* The office is like a family, except that you spend much more time there than with your real family.

In your personal life you have grandmothers, aunts, cousins, sisters; most of us tend to spend more time with our sisters than any of the others. At the office, many women also only want to relate to their office sisters.

But the office is also as dysfunctional a family as your real one, and you get smarter about it by knowing all the people well. Your great-aunt who always causes trouble is not unlike the mischievous secretary who does the same; your grandmother who doles out special favors to her favorite grandkids is exactly like that older woman in sales who does the same. Get to know all these people and their quirks.

- *Enlist anyone who makes sense for the team.* Years ago, when I was a senior executive at CNN, a group of younger women approached me for help getting approval for an on-site day-care center. Their repeated pleas to management had fallen on deaf ears.

Even though my own kids had grown too old for day care, I was happy to do what I could because I had already come to believe that what helped one woman helped all women. So the next time these women met with the head of human resources, he had to deal with someone at his level— me—instead of a group of lower-powered people. Eventually day care became a reality, in part because these young women were smart enough to pick their team carefully.

• • •

Another issue to consider: You must support women at all levels, and, *you must support women at all times.*

Here's a story a woman e-mailed to me after I gave a speech to a group of female accountants:

> At my firm, one of the young women, Erin, started dating a male partner in her section. After they had been seeing each other for a year, she wanted to break up with him, which she ultimately did.
>
> The man was furious. Unfortunately for Erin, he was good friends with the head of her section, who was equally good friends with the managing partner of the office. Not surprisingly, within a short time, Erin was politely asked to leave the firm.
>
> Erin refused. So the firm hired a replacement for her anyway and stopped giving her work. (This was against the company's rules, but that didn't stop them.)
>
> Although she tried to be brave, Erin soon became quite demoralized. She started dressing sloppily; she started coming to work late and leaving early—because she had nothing to do. Simply put, she was giving the partners more reasons for her dismissal.
>
> But the other women at the office rallied around her. One of them sat down with Erin and talked to her about putting on the right show in terms of her appearance and her attitude. Another made sure that she stayed as late as the men by giving her a small amount of work to do each evening.

I then arranged for Erin to be transferred into my department, where we had some real work for her.

All of us provided her with the support that she needed at a point in her career where she could easily have fallen apart and never recovered.

The firm we worked for eventually disintegrated (and I can't say I'm sorry). But several of us, including Erin, joined a better firm, and today she is a very successful partner. She is so good at her job that recently, after she gave birth to twin boys, accountants in our current firm who've never supported part-time arrangements for women have changed their position. Erin will be able to stay with us. So her success is now leading to success for other women in balancing work and family.

• • •

One place where women truly understand teamwork is when one of us is in trouble. We are excellent at supporting each other when something goes wrong, when someone doesn't get the promotion, when the raise doesn't come through. All of a sudden all the other women at the company are our best friends; they're there to say how unfair it was, how they love us, how they support us.

Although women have a fabulous facility for being there in tough times, when life is good, we're the opposite. When a woman is promoted, too often the others no longer consider her part of the team. She's one of "them," no longer one of "us."

I've heard anecdotes that when one woman gets a better job, she isn't interested in the others anymore. "She thinks she's too good for us," her former colleagues say. "She's cut us out."

But I believe that most of the time she's not the one that does the cutting. I think the women who are left behind decide that the Promoted One is no longer a part of their group, and they do more to exclude her than she does to them.

When two women compete for a job, and only one gets it, I promise you that more women will call the one who didn't get it than the one who did (which is the opposite of the male model).

The reality is that the woman who is promoted needs our support more than ever. She's in a new position; she's uncomfortable; she's worried. And on top of that, she's lost her support structure. It's true that her life will be different and she may feel she has to spend time with new people. That's part of how she plays the game on her new level. But that doesn't mean she doesn't want to see you.

We also have to understand that this woman has a lot to teach us. There's usually a good reason she landed the promotion. Let's interact with the one who is successful as well as the one who isn't.

Here's the way it should go: Barbara, a friend of mine at a manufacturing company, recently told me about the time one woman was promoted over her and the other four women in her department. Not all the women thought this woman Andrea was the right choice, and many of them feared that now that she had the Big Job, there would be no room at the top for them. As a result, they resented working for Andrea and several of the women began to denigrate her.

Barbara was horrified by this turn of events. Although she felt that she was the one who should have been promoted, she took the other three women to lunch and discussed the issue openly. Which is better? Barbara asked. Should we all attack Andrea and wound her so badly that she loses her job and the men promote a man, or an outsider, in her place? Or should we become her allies, so she looks good, and we also look good as loyal teammates?

Because these women were basically smart and mature, when presented with such a sensible argument, they were able to see the light. From then on, instead of resenting Andrea, they joined in her success. And when the team prospered, and it was time to hire three more people, Andrea brought two women into the group, making her department the most female friendly in her firm. And, Barbara adds, at some point soon Andrea may well be promoted again, and she is expected to recommend one of the women to replace her.

8
TEAM TIP SIX:
Make Team-Related
Choices

Not long ago, at a financial services company, five different women held positions of power, although none of them was in top management. The women, who had worked together for more than six years, were aware that one day a senior female executive would be named, and one of them would probably rise above the others.

But they also realized that their male bosses were playing each of them off against the other, trying to separate them, asking for confidential information (but these women knew better than to tell tales).

The women's worst fear was that the men would pick someone outside their circle, someone who would not really wield power, but whose name would look good on the annual report.

So the five women got together and after several intense, heated discussions, decided collectively to support the one woman among them whom they most respected and who, once promoted, would do the most good for the other women; she was also the woman they knew the men could accept most easily.

Then they asked one of the five women who was closest to the CEO to tell him gently but firmly about their decision. Understanding that a refusal to accept this choice would create enormous ill will, he acquiesced.

The woman who was selected not only did a great job for the company, she also never forgot her pact with the women who had backed her. She has championed woman-friendly issues and the company has become known for its forward-thinking, enlightened policies.

This may sound like a happily-ever-after fairy tale, but it is a true story. It is, unfortunately, also a rare one.

When you're on a team, you're no longer looking out only for yourself. This has many consequences, but if the team is good—and there's no reason to believe it shouldn't be—those consequences can be very positive ones.

When it looks as though only one woman will be promoted into the male upper circles, it's human nature to want to do everything you can to get the job for yourself. But this is sometimes a counterproductive strategy. Sure, it would be great if one of you steps aside so the most viable candidate can stride forward. That probably won't happen. But you do have to stop yourselves from jeopardizing the chances that any woman will get the job.

In baseball, the batter who hits a sacrifice fly may not have the same satisfaction as the one who gets the home run, but the sacrifice fly can drive in the winning run nonetheless.

We're living in a time where it's all about breakthroughs.

And to achieve those breakthroughs, many of us will have to make a few tactical decisions—for the sake of the women's team. Perhaps you are in a position where you are fighting tooth and nail against another woman for the job above you, and it's clear that only one of you will succeed. How far do you take the battle?

I just saw this happen at a large technology company. There were three competitors for an executive vice president position: two women and one man. The two women were so much smarter and better qualified than the man that they didn't see him as competition, and waged an all out war on each other, recruiting all their allies in the process. They went after each other with such ferocity—creating factions, undermining each other's work, even spreading somewhat malicious gossip—that eventually their bosses, startled by the entire affair, became afraid to hire either of the women. They gave the job to the man.

When it was all over, one of the women confided to me, "If I had known it was going to end like this, I would have backed away. It was important for this company to have a female executive vice president. They've never had one. Now they won't for some time."

Neither of these women, nor their backers, saw the big picture. No one stopped to think about the consequences of their battles. Caught up in the competition, no one asked the two women and their supporters to try to work out a compromise that would have benefited both of them as well as all the other women.

Not that every sacrifice has to be made on such a high level. For example, two friends of mine were once fighting over a client, and it was clear the client didn't know which of them to pick. My fear was that if the battle continued, the client would take the easy road and run off to another firm. My advice to the women: Join forces. Share the client. After realizing that this was probably their only hope for any kind of truce, they came to an agreement. Doing so made both of them look better, and although they had to split the commission, they also split the work and the glory.

Unfortunately, there are no easy answers here. Team-related choices versus individual choices are complicated. There are bound to be situations where your self-interest is such that you are not willing to give. All I am saying is, be aware of the team. Fight for the team as well as for yourself. When you do, you'll open more opportunities for both you and the team.

I'm not pretending that we're all going to put aside our personal ambitions for each other. What a disaster that would be, if we all stopped striving for the best. But why not work together to minimize the potential damage? Competition doesn't rule out cooperation. Blended together, these two concepts can bring out the best in all of us.

Another part of making team-related choices involves remembering that any team is only as good as its weakest link. As mentioned above, we often choose to spend our time and energy with the smartest, most attractive people. We want to help the women we think will become stars; we don't want to be bothered much by the everyday folks who don't appear to be comers.

Help all the women, not just the more obviously gifted. Find time for the request from a woman you think is not-so-gifted. Just because your first impression isn't 100 percent positive doesn't mean you're right. Maybe she's a star who needs your touch to shine. Maybe she's never going to be a star, but she'll become a solid player, and one who will never forget your help.

Consider this: One reason so few women are moving up the ladder is because we tend to find that star, coach her along, and help her land the great job. Then she quits, or she moves on, and we don't have twenty replacements gearing up for action.

That pipeline must be fed. Last month I met with a female school superintendent who recently applied for a new job. The person in charge of taking the applications told her, "We have eighty-five applications so far, and they fall into two categories."

My friend asked what the categories were.

"Eighty-four men," was the response, "and you."

We have to do better. We have to find, and place, more women in the pipeline.

Four team-related points to keep in mind:

1) Don't hold grudges. Give it up for the team, honey. Don't hate someone because she hurt you once. I can't count the number of times a woman has told me something along the lines of: "I will never work with that Katie again. She screwed me out of a contract three years ago."

Some of us can hold a grudge so long that the person we're begrudging doesn't even remember the specifics of what happened—or even that anything happened at all.

Yes, it would be ideal to have harmonious relationships

with all our colleagues and to play on a team where everyone is wonderful. But any team will have people whom you don't want to play with, whom you don't respect. They're still teammates. And as much as you may not like them, their success is, in part, yours too. The more energy you put into negative feelings, the more damage you inflict on the team—and, ultimately, yourself.

It can be unpleasant to play on a team with people whom you don't like. But it makes you smarter. You have to be more strategic; you have to listen more; you have to protect yourself more. These are good skills to hone. You should always want to play with the sharpest, savviest people out there, even though they might not be the nicest.

2) Risk asking your questions in public. I wouldn't be so aware of this if I didn't give so many speeches. The minute the speech ends and I walk to the ladies' room, several dozen women are upon me with a barrage of questions.

Women don't like to stand up and ask a personal question. We prefer a private consultation. It's safer. After all, you never know what the answer could be. What if it reveals too much about you?

But an important team-related choice (particularly in this day and age where we go to so many seminars, lectures, and speeches) is to ask the question in front of the other women so they can benefit from the answer.

Men are much more willing to ask questions in a public forum—particularly if they think the speaker is smart. The better the speaker, the less likely a woman is to ask a question, because she wants a private audience.

If you don't ask about what's on your mind, you don't help the group (or yourself). Part of being on the team is helping each other learn. The more open you are, the more knowledge can be shared.

3) *Tell someone if her self-presentation is distracting.* This can be truly difficult. I know this firsthand, because I did it for that woman who wore white shoes at the wrong time. It's challenging, but so many women have told me how great it was that someone let them know that they shouldn't wear those huge dangling earrings when making a speech, or that their skirts were too short, or that they absently tapped their fingers too loudly during meetings.

The easiest way to avoid embarrassment is to wait until the two of you are alone. Begin the sentence with a positive reinforcement, such as, "Julie, you are an excellent presenter—but you would be even better if you weren't wearing such distracting jewelry."

We're uncomfortable commenting on another woman's appearance because we wonder if it's really our business. But it is, if we're a genuine team player. If we see a colleague about to make a mistake in a business context, it's our obligation to say something. Making team-related choices means speaking the truth, even when you know people won't like what you have to say. It's wrong only if you are being a busybody or just plain nasty.

4) *If you're in a position of power, do what you can to use that power.* Here's a story from a local television station in the West. Two women had a problem: Both women were excellent producers, but they were also married with several children, and neither wanted a full-time job. Yet they both needed to work to help support their families.

These women were very smart, because instead of simply asking their boss, Marie, for advice or help, they mapped out a thorough strategy: The two of them wrote out a well-documented proposal showing how they could share one job and produce an hour of television daily, and, their plan wouldn't cost the company an extra cent.

Everyone's first reaction was doubt. How could the woman who worked on Monday know what the other one was planning for Friday? What if specific questions arose and the wrong woman was at the helm at the wrong time? But these producers had taken everything into consideration and their plan accounted for all possible problems.

The power structure opposed the idea, but because Marie saw a chance to give these women an opportunity not just to support their families, but to show that flexibility could profit the company, she convinced the power structure that they should try it—and it worked.

(By the way, being smart is an important part of the equation. Don't just complain about how the office refuses to accommodate your family schedule. Find a way to fix it. Be proactive. Come up with your own ideas. These women had a problem, but they solved it by inviting other friends on the team to talk over ideas until they were able to draw up a plan that was hard to resist.)

TEAM TIP SEVEN:
Weave a Female Web

Shannon, in her late thirties, had been working at a large Los Angeles–based accounting firm for six years when her twin daughters were born. Shannon is ambitious, but she wanted to stay at home until her girls entered elementary school.

When I met her at a speech I gave for female accountants, she'd returned to her old company and had been back on the career track for the last four years. Like many women, Shannon came up after the speech ended to ask her question. (As always, I told her that next time she should ask it aloud so the other women could hear her concerns.)

Because she had taken time off (and because she's somewhat shy), Shannon felt she didn't know enough women in her business. She understood the importance of networking, but she was unsure how to meet more female colleagues. She also said that the way the men networked left her cold— she never felt comfortable going to large conferences and meetings, handing out thousands of cards to total strangers, shaking hands with women she knew she'd never meet again. It all seemed too impersonal, she said.

Since I knew a single mother who was about to move to the same neighborhood in which Shannon lives, I asked a few questions about her life there. Shannon turned out to be a remarkable resource; she knew the best day care, the best baby-sitters, the best dry cleaner. I told her I would pass along the information to my friend, along with her name.

Then I asked her how she had accumulated all this excellent data. Through friends, she replied.

Well, I asked, how would she feel about mixing those friends into her business life? Maybe they needed accounting. Maybe their husbands did. Maybe they had other friends who knew friends, and so on.

Shannon shook her head. "It wouldn't be right to ask them about business," she said.

"You mean," I asked, "it's only okay to ask them questions about your personal needs?" And when she nodded uncertainly, I told her unequivocally why this was not a helpful way to think. Shannon had a large network waiting to be tapped, but she didn't want to tap it.

In the last decade many women have come to believe that the word "networking" has a negative connotation, implying some sort of impersonal form of connection in which we attend events, pretend we are interested in every woman we meet, pass out our business cards, and leave feeling as though (a) we have accomplished nothing and (b) we weren't true to ourselves.

Forget networking. What we really need to be doing is

what I call *webbing*. (I am indebted to journalist and business consultant Sally Helgeson and her excellent book *Web of Inclusion* for inspiration on this topic.) We need to create interlocking webs that cross every facet of our lives, webs that are genuinely connected together and shored up whenever possible.

Years ago I'd attend a business event, meet someone interesting, have an intimate conversation, and never follow through. I knew the two of us could become friends given the right circumstances, but I was also perfectly happy with these one-night stands. I thought a relationship was something that required daily nurturing. And that is, indeed, one kind of relationship. But having a great evening with a friend whom you don't see again until the next time your paths cross is just as viable a relationship—it just has a different feel to it.

Such relationships must become the very fabric of our existence, and a very natural fabric at that (more like Egyptian cotton than polyester). When fabrics are well used, they no longer feel false or stiff. They feel comfortable and inviting.

Historically women have tended to say, "I have my business life and I have my personal life," or, "These are people I know from the office; these are friends from home." We're so busy trying to keep everything separate, and we think the men are crazy for having one life—the guys they play golf with are the guys they do business with.

The truth is, we don't have two lives called "home" and "business," one natural and one artificial. It's all one life now. After all, we live in a world where we work from our homes using computers and modems, where we pack our BlackBerries when we travel, where the phrase "twenty-four-seven" no longer applies just to convenience stores. We're almost always connected to work, no matter where we are. Our life is a blend of what used to be considered life's two separate components: what we do and who we are.

Things were different in our parents' era. My dad knew people from his career and people outside his career. These were different groups and never the twain met. Today, as I put together a list of guests for my daughter's upcoming wedding, I can see that once-clear lines are now blurry—people move frictionlessly and seamlessly from personal to professional life and back again.

My ex-husband and I traveled to China the first year it opened up to Americans, and on this overly organized trip we met two other couples with whom we became immediate friends, as we were all rather boisterous. One of those women was a struggling young banker named Susan Ness, just as I was a struggling young employee at CNN. Based on this unusual trip together, we decided to stay connected, and once a year we phoned each other just to check in. Flash forward: The year I became executive vice president of CNN, Susan was appointed a commissioner at the Federal Communications Commission. Today she is Distinguished Visiting Professor at the Annenberg School at the University of Pennsylvania, and Director, Information and Society, of the Annenberg Public Policy Center.

My initial connection to Susan had nothing to do with business. We were simply friends. But we stayed in touch because we liked each other and knew that some day we would connect again over business.

I know that not every woman has this kind of ease. That's

why some of you have to work at it every day. That's why you join the appropriate network. Become known within your industry. Reconnect your relationship with one or two of the people in your web.

But here's the key: You do not do these things in manipulative ways. You do them as a genuine expression of yourself.

I remember walking out of a restaurant in Washington a few years ago and hearing someone say, "Aren't you Gail Evans?" I turned around to see a woman who looked vaguely familiar. She reintroduced herself and I remembered her from our college days. We then talked at some length and discovered a connecting thread; I worked for CNN while she was the chief lobbyist for the National Cable & Telecommunications Association. Needless to say, right then and there we had both shored up our webs—and become useful connections for each other. That's something women have much more difficulty comprehending than men.

A good web is made of a million different kinds of people, many of whom you hear from constantly, others whom you haven't had contact with in years. One is no less a part of your web than the other.

Make these connections happen. For example, there are always certain women at work who seem to be the ones who say, "Sara's getting engaged; I'll give her a shower." These shower-givers aren't just being thoughtful, and these showers aren't just about socializing. They are opportunities to meet new women from related fields (as well as to show appreciation for your fellow workers). If you give these parties, you start strengthening your network, because such events help smooth out working relationships as people get to know each other in a softer environment, allowing them to appear more human, able to reveal sides of their personalities they might be reluctant to show at the office.

Likewise, when you attend a dinner party, you're not just meeting other people in a social context, you are potentially meeting business contacts: men and women whom you may end up asking for a job someday, or offering a job to, or engaging in some business transaction.

Let me tell you three short stories from three different generations of women. Just the other night I got a phone call from a friend's daughter whom I didn't know well—I didn't even know what she did for a living. She was calling out of the blue because she had met me at a dinner a few months earlier and knew that I might be able to help her with a particularly confusing office situation. Her father is a successful businessman, but she didn't turn to him because her problem was female related and she wanted a woman's reaction. Good for her! She took a social introduction and turned it into an opportunity to solicit advice.

Going back a few years, an old friend of my in-laws called me regarding her granddaughter who had just graduated from college. "I want her to work in an interesting environment with a smart, supportive woman," she said. "Can I bring her down to Georgia so you can meet her, and if there's a job opening, you might hire her—and maybe even mentor her?" Although I barely remembered this woman, I knew my in-laws respected her and I liked the way she handled the call; she was honest and forthright. A month later the two women flew to Atlanta, and because the granddaughter was everything her grandmother said she was, I soon hired her. She remained at CNN for a good twenty years.

And in a generational shift, another acquaintance called me—this time about her mother, Irene, who at sixty was going through a rough divorce. Irene needed money, as well as something to do so she could feel good about herself, but she hadn't worked in thirty-five years. I agreed to talk to her on the phone, and found her unusually smart and engaging. So I called all the women I knew who would understand the situation and asked them how to help Irene restart her life. We soon discovered that she had done volunteer work for years and was a superb organizational specialist. Since one of the big catering firms in the city needed a detail person for their large parties, they met her, hired her, and ten years later, Irene is still going strong.

• • •

For too long women have thought that the group is not important, that it's the individual who counts, that we can make it solely on our own merits. But think about the remarkable power of the group. Think of what men have already achieved using groups. And remember: You do not have to give up your individuality when you become part of the group. You can enhance it.

After all, we have always been comfortable establishing informal webs that revolve around family life—the car-pool mothers, the play group, etc. Here you can find out about a new baby-sitter, a good cleaning service, or a discount grocery store.

Women must establish their business webs with equal assurance. It doesn't have to be through the traditional male routes, like the poker game or the after-work beer. We can do it any way we wish, such as casual lunches at the cafeteria, morning coffee at the local café, or an after-work exercise class. The type of forum doesn't matter. Having the forum does.

When you go to an event, don't go with the purpose of handing out your card; go with the purpose of meeting interesting people and getting fresh ideas for your life. That way, handing out a business card will feel natural, not artificial. Talk with the people you meet about your real life and your genuine concerns, not about some made-up business issue that neither of you cares about. And don't feel everyone you meet has to have best-friend potential. Casual contacts can lead to powerful opportunities.

How often do your hear a man say that he plays tennis with the guy he just closed the deal with, or that he met the lawyer the company wants to hire in the cigar room after dinner?

You simply never know where the next opportunity will arise. Here's a story someone who read my first book e-mailed to me as I was writing this chapter: Kelly is a young woman who recently took a job at a Texas technology company. She hates networking events because they seem so artificial, but she forces herself to go to as many as she can stomach, scouring the room for contacts, although she really isn't sure what she's looking for.

One night she was sitting at a business dinner next to an interesting woman who looked about twenty-five years her senior. The woman, Virginia, was telling Kelly how much she resembled her daughter. At first Kelly thought she was simply wasting her time because the conversation had little to do with business. But the more they talked, the more Kelly began to enjoy herself. Soon they were talking as friends.

Virginia was at the dinner only because she was in town visiting her sister and had agreed to accompany her to this event. She admitted she knew little about technology, but she was interested in hearing about Kelly's job. Kelly explained the technology behind the software her company had developed, doing her best to make it comprehensible to a woman who had only recently started using a personal computer.

When she finished, Virginia commented that her brother-in-law was the chairman of a company in a related field and that she thought he might be interested in hearing about this software. The next day, Kelly sent her company's information to Virginia, who forwarded it to the brother-in-law, who immediately set up a meeting with Kelly's firm. Within a month she had concluded a solid sale.

• • •

There are many, many ways to build your web. The following suggestions are only the beginning:

• *Actively nurture your relationships.* Whatever ways you decide to build and use your networks, keep in mind that it's an ongoing process of outreach and maintenance.

Send a note, an e-mail, or a present when a baby is born, a promotion is received, or a tough job is completed. Clip an article and send it to someone you know who could use it. Make sure you don't only connect when you need something. Even when I do need a favor, I connect on a personal basis a few days before I make my request. Is this manipulative? Perhaps, but if you simply treat people exactly as you wish to be treated yourself, you won't repeatedly question your motives.

• *Network wherever you go.* When the guys watch their kids play soccer, they'll stand on the sidelines and yell, but they'll also talk about what happened when Joe's firm merged with Sam's. Life and work—they're blended together. The guy who meets a stockbroker at the pro shop at the golf course is not shocked when the other man calls him the next week to solicit his business.

Women tend to resist this kind of networking. I know one sophisticated women's group where one member gave out other members' names to her certified financial planner (CFP). This woman thought her CFP friend was excellent and wanted to help her. Apparently over two hundred e-mails flew back and forth after that original note. The outrage! The violation! How could anyone dare to transgress privacy in such a flagrant fashion! But what did this woman really do? She was simply helping a friend by giving out business (not personal) numbers, just as men do all the time. For too long we have acted as though a wall existed between our personal and our professional lives. It doesn't.

Last year I went to grandparents' day at one of my grandsons' nursery schools and had a wonderful time, learned a great deal about my grandson's school life, and returned home with an excellent offer to give a speech. While I was there a friend told me that she'd read my last book, and a woman who overheard us introduced herself and explained that, as the head of a secretarys' day event for the American Heart Association, she had been looking for a speaker. My name had come up, but she didn't know me. Now she did.

I'm not saying that no matter where you are, you should network. Just be able to realize a potential opportunity when you see one—and not because you plotted it. It never entered my mind that a speaking opportunity would come out of grandparents' day. It just naturally grew out of the conversations I was having.

Networking is about contact. Who is the person you hire to be your lawyer, to rebuild your roof, whatever? Often it's the person you just had contact with. You don't go through a million names every time you might need someone. One day you meet someone who's in the paving business, and you remember your driveway is a total mess. She says her firm does these kind of jobs routinely, and voilà! Business is being done.

- *Look for multiple ways to connect with everyone you meet.* Many women have started forming non-work-related groups that help them connect. At one Atlanta-based company, a dozen women formed a reading group, and another dozen formed an investment club. At a St. Louis law firm, the secretaries created a baby-sitting co-op; each of them can have one weekend night out every three weeks in exchange for baby-sitting someone else's children.

If you don't work at a large company, all the more reason to form strong ties—I know a freelance journalist who's such an avid weekend hiker that she has formed a female writers outdoors club that takes day-hikes once every six weeks, and one long weekend every year.

Think up ideas. Be inventive. If you've got kids, what about that woman you met at your daughter's camp, or the nursery school carpool, or at the checkout line at the grocery store? These people can all be contacts for you. Maybe that nice mother with the twins isn't working now, but she used to be an events planner for a major hotel chain. Maybe she'll be back at work in a few years and remember you.

If you're a single, what about forming a travel club so you can go to all those exotic places you've never felt comfortable going to alone? You can share expenses, have fun, and get to know a workmate in a new way.

I used to do aqua aerobics. Invariably the other women in my classes had interesting careers—one owned a printing business, another was a nurse, another a part-time caterer. I would bet that over the years almost all of us have done some form of business together.

- **Be inclusive.** As mentioned, the cleaning crew is part of the team too. Don't put all of your focus upward. Nearly everyone has something to teach, including the mail-room clerk and the security guard. Unless we're related to the boss, we all start at the bottom. *Playboy* magazine founder Hugh Hefner's daughter Christie once said that the key to her success was genetics. Most of us don't have genetics on our side.

- **You're never too important to network.** After they get promoted, many women say, "Now I have to isolate myself." Or,

"I can't be involved in office friendships because I'll make decisions that affect my friends." Or, "The guys will think less of me if I spend time with people at a lower level."

This is a convoluted belief that the more successful you become, the more distance you must put between yourself and other women. Actually, the opposite is true: The more important you get, the more essential it is to be accessible to other women. Not only will you help the women's team move along, the team will help and support you. (And do you think the guys don't help each other?)

Perhaps one reason we lose steam as we get closer to the top is this self-imposed isolation. We keep telling ourselves, "I'm the only woman in the room." Then we accept it, instead of putting energy into getting another woman in the room too.

But when we have these sets of supportive women in our lives, being the only woman in the room is no longer lonely, because there are a thousand women who are the only woman in the room. It's only lonely because so many of us say it is. There is powerful relationship potential when you meet another woman who is the only woman in her room as well.

- *Think quantity as well as quality.* The more people you know, even in a very casual way, the easier it is for you to move the action. Though the good old boys have their small circle with concentrated power, women rarely find the new job through just one quick source. It's much more apt to be that you heard from an acquaintance that a friend's sister has an opening that might be perfect for you.

- *Take advantage of male sensibilities.* Some of your best opportunities may come from the men, although they may not be aware of it. For instance, if a group of men are arranging an important meeting with a new client and they find out there's a woman on the other team, they'll often scurry around to find a woman for their team too. Suddenly you're invited.

Many women become irritated when this occurs because they feel like they're being displayed like a show poodle. Don't take offense—take advantage. The other woman is usually at your level or higher, and has some real power, or she wouldn't be there. If you connect and bond with her, you will help your company, and yourself.

- *Keep growing.* Look for groups and people with skills and intelligence you don't have. Join groups where you expand your information base, not ones where you keep reinforcing what you already know.

- *Be prepared.* When people ask, "What do you do?" you need a good one-line answer.

Most women don't have one. Being coy about yourself may have worked in your sophomore year of high school. It doesn't work now.

Years ago, when asked what she did for a living, television personality Greta Van Susteren used to hem and haw and say that she worked in a law firm. Most people assumed she was a paralegal. Actually, she was a founding partner, but she felt uncomfortable admitting that. How many men would feel so uncomfortable?

Just yesterday, as I was about to do a radio interview, the

host introduced me as a former vice president of CNN. I corrected her by saying, pleasantly but firmly, that I was the former *executive* vice president. This forced me into uncomfortable territory, because I felt a little obnoxious. But what's the advantage of selling ourselves short? If you are senior accountant or director of an accounting department, don't just say that you're an accountant. Be proud of that extra title. You probably worked very hard to get it. Why let someone else take it away from you?

Every time we speak up and acknowledge our achievement, we make it easier for all women to get the respect we deserve, and have fought so hard to get.

- *Don't forget the Internet.* Research shows that for most men, the Internet is like the workplace. They log on; they discover what they were looking for; they're gone. But because of our orientation toward relationships, women tend to see being online as a more social phenomenon.

One of the Internet's greatest qualities is its fast access to intimacy—you can create a relationship very quickly. And the resulting e-mail is very validating. The more e-mail we get, the more we know that people are thinking about us. I've seen many women who, when having a bad day, perk up when a good e-mail (or two or three) arrives.

But keep the e-mail you receive at work at a professional level. This means avoiding the smiley faces, the cute expressions, the poor grammar, and those icons and exclamation points that indicate an e-mail is important when it isn't. Acceptable when corresponding with friends, they are not acceptable in workplace communication.

The Internet allows us all to obtain more input from other members of the team. Talk to each other through e-mail. Go to women's sites—especially those that answer business questions. For instance, you can uncover information that can seem off-limits in conversation. Women are often in the dark about negotiating raises; often this is because we don't know our coworkers' salaries. So go to www.salary.com, which features a chart that shows what people who live or work in your zip code are making—just the kind of specific information you need when you go in to talk with your supervisor.

Enter chat rooms where you can find out what other women are thinking and doing. Solve problems. You already use the computer for the home—if your mother becomes sick, you find a site for her illness. Apply that model to the business world.

The computer is a larger version of the phone, a device invented for business use but which women used to form relationships. We just need to warm up to it.

• *Remember that networking is never short term.* Your friends from high school are still potential networkers for you when you're sixty years old. You're never too old to connect.

• *Have fun.* A rose is a rose is a rose . . . and a job is a job is a job. Women must stop ascribing high significance to everything that happens at work. It's okay to tell a joke or laugh at someone else's between nine and five. It's okay to lighten up about our fellow employees and allow ourselves to like and enjoy them, even when they're not perfect. Having a network of women you trust and who make you laugh is a powerful way to ease up those parts of work that can feel like a burden.

Enjoy the company picnic, or bowling league, or softball team. Go to the company park clean-up day thinking you'll have an adventure. Find women who make you smile. Part of being in a network is having fun with your fellow network-ers. The best networks are those where someone tells a story about some work-related event, and everyone else bursts into uncontrollable laughter.

Smart people bring a velvet glove to the office, not a steel one.

• • •

The traditional man's network was always epitomized by that big, impersonal Rolodex filled with names of people whom the boss knew nothing about except perhaps their title.

Your network is different. It's composed of all the women you've met in your life whom you genuinely want to remember—a teacher, a banker, a schoolmate. Together they compose a new kind of web, not a how-do-I-use-this-person-to-get-ahead network, but an I-like-this-person-and-would-love-to-work-with-her one. It's relationship-oriented and that's why it is female.

Be smart enough to know that at least some of those names may be valuable in your professional as well as your personal life. Don't do that female thing that says, "We're just friends; I can't interfere with our relationship by con-necting it to business." Of course you can. It doesn't violate the friendship. It helps both of you, and by doing that, you both help make the team stronger.

PART 3

Challenges of the Team

10
Twelve Team Members to Watch Out For

The other day I had lunch with Kathy, an executive vice president at a Seattle-area company, and one of two women with that title in her company. She is in sales. The other woman, Suzanne, is in marketing. Kathy has been at her firm for more than twenty years and is an excellent player on both the company team and the women's team. She loves her job, but she has a problem at work, and it's not with the men, who have been solicitous of her opinions and enjoy having her on board.

Her problem is with Suzanne, who didn't come up through the ranks but was recently brought into the company from the outside, and who tends to position herself both internally and publicly as the highest ranking woman. She also implies publicly that she's the only female executive vice president.

Suzanne claims to be on the women's team. She gives frequent interviews about her meteoric rise, talking about the importance of female mentors and why all women must help one another. Yet by refusing to talk about how wonderful it is to have two women at her level, Suzanne is hurting the women's team.

My advice to Kathy: Talk to Suzanne. Try to get her to understand that the two of you are in this together. But keep it light. Take her to a nice lunch and drop hints that you know what's going on—but make sure she knows you enjoy having her around. Suggest that you work together—ask her if she'd like to create a dog-and-pony show the public relations people can use to prove the company has female-friendly policies. Invite Suzanne to come along the next time you're asked to do an interview. Get her to understand that the fact there are two of you makes her just as powerful, if not more so.

My guess is that Suzanne has never had to deal with another woman as successful as she is, and it might take her some time to be willing to share the spotlight. But when she does, she will realize that in numbers there is strength.

• • •

Not every woman will play on the women's team. Even those who say they always do, often don't. While the vast majority of the women you will meet in work and in life are perfectly nice, you must be aware of the ones who have the potential to hurt you. The following is a field guide to help you spot them in their natural habitat.

Let's say you've started working at a company called DGSA, a midsize corporation that specializes in diverse gen-

Gail Evans

eral services, and you're a diverse general services associate. It's a good post, and you're happy to have it.

DGSA is mildly progressive when it comes to women's issues, and the company has recently attempted to increase the number of women in senior positions. Furthermore, with a few committed female colleagues, you've helped start the DGSA Women's Forum, which meets once a month.

You like the other women who have joined your group and you're hopeful that together you will make a difference. You feel committed to the DGSA team objectives as well as the women's team objectives.

But just because most of the DGSA women seem agreeable and sympathetic doesn't necessarily mean all of them are. Not only do you have to consider all the roadblocks that the men throw up in front of you, you must consider the various women who never seem to be part of the team. These people can be as obstructive as the men, if you aren't able to recognize who they are, and take adequate precautions.

For instance, down the hall from you is *Helen Hoarder*, who just got promoted. You've been assigned to her old job.

Helen is a lovely woman, but she has a problem. Whenever Helen gets promoted from an old job to a new one, she fails to understand that her new job is now her *only* job, and that part of her task is to help the woman who replaced her—in this case, you—do her old job well.

But Helen, who was secure doing the old job, is insecure in the new one, and she can't let go. She stops you from performing well because she's always in your office, explaining to you exactly how she did it, expecting you to do it similarly.

She is clear that it's easier for her to do it herself than to teach you what to do. Helen hurts the women's team because she hoards all the work for herself, which means that the women below her don't get a chance to grow.

Personally, when I was promoted I couldn't wait to get rid of what I used to do, because I was bored and ready to move on.

Maybe one reason women have such difficulty breaking through the glass ceiling is because we are so comfortable with our feet stuck in the cement. To break through you have to be willing to get rid of that secure footing. I know several women who could have fought to become the presidents of their companies, but they never did. They wanted to stay where they felt safe. And the boys were hardly going to advance them unless they were willing to battle for those top jobs.

I used to run into Helen Hoarders constantly, the women who would always be sitting in their offices late at night after their staff had gone home. When I would ask a Helen why she was still there, she would explain that one of her staff was sick, another didn't fully understand the job yet, another wasn't sharp enough, and most of all, none of them could do the job as well as she could. She has all the knowledge, and frankly, that's really the way she wants to keep it.

If you were to complain to me about Helen, I would probably recommend that you consider looking for work elsewhere. Helen is a dead-end street, and you missed the Do Not Enter sign. All you're going to learn here is how to be like her, and you don't want to become a young Helen Hoarder.

You also must deal with the woman in the office next

door to Helen, *Alice Acrophobia,* who suffers from a related problem. Like Helen, Alice feels insecure. She has been promoted higher than she ever expected, and she fears these heights. Unlike Helen, Alice is willing to let go of her old job. But she's insecure because she doesn't really believe she deserves, or can do, her new job.

Alice suffers from what is known as impostor syndrome—the horrible feeling that your success is accidental and that at any minute your inadequacies will be publicly exposed. Women who suffer from impostor syndrome frequently expend as much energy trying to figure out how to survive their presumed unmasking as they expend on their actual job.

The guy across from Alice who got the same promotion assumes that the Big Bosses wouldn't have put him there if they didn't have faith in him. But Alice can't see it that way. She'd prefer that safe piece of cement below her feet.

Most men believe they are promoted because of their potential. Women believe their promotion is due to their performance. In other words, men assume they got their new position because they are capable of doing more than their last job, whereas women assume they got the new job because of their achievement.

But then a Helen or an Alice also thinks: "What if I can't do this new job? In fact, what happens if they find out I didn't do the last job as well as they think?" They capsize their futures by deciding that the promotion was a mistake, instead of trusting the bosses enough to understand they had a good reason for the promotions.

With a woman like Alice, you simply have to be careful and patient. Until she can gather her wits about her and accept that she earned her promotion, she is going to be capricious and unreliable, hardly a major asset to the team. In the meantime you can help Alice by helping her calm down, by letting her know that you are there to catch her if she falls.

And of course, you can learn from Alice's mistakes. She's a great negative role model—she shows you how not to behave.

Sitting in the office around the corner from you is *Polly Perfect*. Polly is a smart woman, but she never stops trying to do everything right. Polly learned in school that studying hard and pleasing the teacher brought good grades and accolades, and she still brings that attitude to work every day. Polly feels that only by doing everything exactly and completely right can she honestly believe that she is doing her job well.

One of the most common complaints you hear from Polly Perfect is how "certain people around here" get away with murder. Usually she is referring to the creative people—the unpredictable types who come through in the clutch, but who aren't always easy to work with, who don't turn out dependable and predictable results.

What Polly doesn't understand is that being on a team doesn't mean that everyone operates the same way. Personally, I don't happen to share Polly's belief that getting things just right is the only way. A team has many members, some perfectionists, some creative. The goal is to do *your* best job, the best way you know how. Don't listen to Polly Perfect if she tells you that you, too, have to be perfect. Maybe your best skill is your ability to come up with inventive insights.

That's a valuable tool, and one that can't be judged on a scale of bad to perfect.

In the office next to her Polly has a close friend and ally named *Elizabeth Expert*. Elizabeth is the technical expert on any given field or piece of equipment. Here at DGSA she is an expert on the company's number one product, the Dag-saw, and she knows more about it than anyone else.

But when Elizabeth is promoted, her new job is no longer about the ins and outs of that complicated equipment. It's about motivating others to do their best and getting the team to work together. Because Elizabeth is the expert, however, she stays focused on her old skill set, instead of the new one. She concentrates on her knowledge instead of her people.

What neither Elizabeth nor Polly can see is that there is more to a job than getting everything just right. I read a study recently that says men tend to increase their job skills by attending company-sponsored classes on how to be lead-ers, whereas women prefer spending their own money and going out-of-house to universities to be better informed about the material they're working with. In other words, the man wants to learn how to be a boss; the woman wants to learn how to become an expert. She keeps getting promoted based on her expertise, while he is promoted on his ability to handle people. Ultimately the Big Boss is the one who can handle people.

You have to watch out for both Polly and Elizabeth. You don't want to get caught being part of their group because they can't see beyond it. Like Helen and Alice, they won't help you grow.

Down the hall from these women is *Olivia Overwhelmed*. Hopefully Olivia will never be your boss because she wouldn't be good at guiding anyone, including herself. Her desk is stacked with papers, her office is littered with files, her life is filled with complications.

One of the qualities you most want in a boss is the ability to help you see how your own career can take off. Olivia would never have time for you or any other employee because she's trying so hard to keep all her balls in the air. "I'd love to help you," she says. "But I've got too much work."

Actually, Olivia doesn't have that much work. She just needs to think she does, because she's not comfortable unless she's drowning.

To deal with Olivia: Engage her in a helpful, focused conversation. Sit down and say, "You seem to have so much going on. Maybe I can help if I take this, or if Henrietta Helpful takes that, or we can find someone else to divide the work. We are here for you. We want to support you." That's what Olivia needs to hear, and she may be grateful when you say it. But don't count on it: She also may be too busy to hear anything.

A little farther down the corridor sits *Silent Treatment Sophie*, who is truly dangerous. Sophie is still playing games from her childhood. She believes that sometime in the past a coworker did her wrong, and she can never forgive her. Whenever this woman is around, Sophie gives her the silent treatment, or rolls her eyes, or even makes a nasty face.

I once had a colleague who didn't speak to one of her office mates for a full year, which meant that everyone else had to cope with the situation. That made all of us feel silly, especially when the two women were in the same room.

You must be careful around Sophie—not because she has real power, but because she can make you nuts. You keep thinking that if you act normally it will all go away, but Sophie wants to hold on to it forever.

Best friends with Sophie is *Diane Drama*. Diane is that woman who's never happy unless there's a catastrophe in the making. She gossips up a storm about the bosses, and as soon as something goes wrong for you at work, she's in your face telling you how justifiable your anger is and how angry she is for you. She reminds you of all the things Big Boss has done in the past to spite you, and she loves getting you even more worked up than you were before she came along.

Diane is easy to spot: She hates newcomers at the office (until they become part of her gossip network) and she always eats lunch with the same people. Her favorite saying is, "I told you so."

Stay away from Diane! She'll never help you figure out effective strategies. Her advice consists of such nonstarters as "You should just quit," or "Go tell the boss's boss and really get even."

Diane doesn't really want you to do well. In fact, your demise is her pleasure. She wants you to become fodder for more gossip. Right after you're fired for mouthing off, she's telling everyone what a shame it is, neglecting to mention that it was on her advice.

You and I know that men are gossips too, but they don't get hooked by the same kind of gossipmongers as women do. They blow off the Diane Dramas of the world because they are clear she has no real power. But to women, especially the younger ones, Diane looks and sounds like she knows everything, because her stories are so office-focused. Girls want to fit in, and when Diane embraces you, it can be tempting.

Resist temptation. Be pleasant to Diane and wish her well, but she is ultimately depressing, and no one will be impressed with your association.

On the floor above these women, sitting with the higher-ups, is *Irene Intimidator*.

Unfortunately, Irene learned most of her management skills from the men, and she decided that the only way to get ahead was to become a stronger version of the overly aggressive guys she has worked with. Fearing that people would find her weak if she didn't show her alpha-male side, she has become a take-no-prisoners boss who believes that scaring people is the best way to motivate them. She yells; she bullies; she pushes; she basically makes your life miserable.

If a woman is insecure about her leadership abilities, it's easy for her to fall back on being nasty and difficult for a certain period of time. And it does get results—just not ones that last over the long haul.

How do you deal with Irene Intimidator? Show her that you are supportive of her being boss, and help her see it's fine to be her natural self and not a pseudomale. If you're kind to Irene, she may calm down and stop feeling that she has to be intimidating in order to command your attention.

Keep in mind: Most of us know what we will tolerate from male bosses. We can usually handle it when they yell and scream—after all, we expect them to yell and scream. That's what men do. But when a woman does the same, she contradicts our preconceived concepts of how women should act. We are expected to be more relationship oriented, more caring, more thoughtful. We aren't permitted to show the dark side.

The result is a double standard. When a woman is unusually aggressive, we feel she isn't a good boss. Whenever I lost my cool and yelled, my female staffers went crazy. "Gail isn't supposed to do that," they'd say. Yet these women tolerated men who acted like maniacs.

Try not to judge other women more harshly than you do the men. If Irene Intimidator infuriates you, but you can put up with everything Stanley Screamer doles out, understand that you are being unfair.

Up on the bosses' floor is *Queen Bea*. Not so common as she used to be, Queen Bea is that one woman in the inner circle, and she has fallen in love with her role. Usually a little older, Queen Bea is probably less knowledgeable about business matters than some of the younger women. This makes her feel threatened. Where these women can't match her is her knowledge of the company's history and where all the bodies are buried (which makes those skill sets even more important to Bea).

Queen Bea didn't advance up the corporate ladder the same way the younger ones are doing it. The odds are good she's there because the men felt they had to let a woman into the inner circle, and they wanted someone who wouldn't be trouble. A lot of the younger women aren't as easy to figure out. Queen Bea is nothing if not predictable.

But even though the men around her end up being younger as the years go on, Bea is an institution. She's not going to get knocked off, not at her age, and she knows it. And she is not one of those *Oprah*-inspired women who get to a certain point and say, "This has been a great ride. What can I try next?" For Bea, it isn't a ride. It's her life. It's a foregone conclusion that she will die in the job.

In a way, the Queen Beas of the world are not unlike the guys in that they probably don't have children, and may not even be married.

Watch out for Bea. Because she loves her position of being the only woman, she can't be counted on to help you or any other woman share her space or make her less indispensable.

The best way to deal with Queen Bea is to become her ally. Admire her knowledge of the company. Marvel at her institutional savvy. Bea can even be likable once you get to know her. And, she can teach you a lot.

Above all, if you need to know something from the hierarchy, go to Bea first. Never go over her head or let her hear you were talking to one of the Big Guys without her knowledge. At the end of a conversation, you add, "Should I talk to Boss Bob about this?" And Bea responds, "Yes, that wouldn't be a bad idea." Asking that one question can mean the difference between success and failure with Bea. And there's no point making an enemy of her, because if you do, you may spend the rest of your career regretting it.

Just below Queen Bea on the totem pole is *Seniority Sue*. She, too, has been at the job forever and knows the company backward and forward. But unlike Bea, Sue hasn't made it into the inner circle. Recently she even started reporting to a younger woman who is twice as knowledgeable about the job. But Sue believes the most important part of her résumé is how many years she's logged at the company, and the knowledge that comes from all those years.

Sue resents how much money that young woman is making. Her belief is that a person's salary should be based on years at the company—no more, no less.

The reason that her boss makes more than Sue does is that at DGSA, like most organizations, many people perform similar tasks. The younger woman was put out that the older women who do the same job take twice as long to do it, and so she went to the boss and complained. "If I don't get more money," she said, "I'm gone."

She got her raise, because she has the skills that demand higher compensation. But Seniority Sue then asks, "What is all my seniority worth if you give my salary to someone who has only been here six years?"

Sue is a good, solid worker, but she's reached a point where she's barely worth her salary. She's frustrated because she knows she's not going anywhere. And, she sees that many of the younger, smart women are jumping over women like her. She is angry, both looking down and looking up.

You must be very careful of Seniority Sue because she usually has a direct pipeline to the bosses. She has known them forever. She was there when the Big Boss got married; she's friendly with his wife; she sends his kids birthday cards; she even knows the family dog. So when Sue decides she

?

doesn't like you, she can use her access in subtle ways. She doesn't need to go one level above you. She goes four levels above you.

Now, Sue doesn't have the power to hurt you directly. She does have the power to undermine you, to raise questions about your work. Are you really competent? Are you really doing a good job? She raises these questions with the Big Boss, who then asks his second, who then continues asking them, all the way down to your immediate supervisor, who now wonders too.

It's hard to find the right strategy to cope with Seniority Sue. She's insecure, and for good reason. As a younger woman with great potential, you threaten her. The best you can do is form a relationship with her where you make it clear that you won't fire her if you're ever promoted over her. And a pleasant word now and then won't hurt. Stop by her office and say hello. Tell her you're going to the break room and ask if she needs anything. She needs to feel important. Remember her birthday or even better, her anniversary with the company. It might not make her like you, but it might make her day—and safeguard your career.

Another friend of Bea and Sue is *Punishing Patty*, who has a certain quirk. If you come on overly strong, Patty will find a way to hurt you. She dislikes strength. The guys tend to punish people who are weak. But Patty feels much more comfortable with quiet, meek women. She wants to give these women a chance and sticks up for them with their superiors (who have probably never noticed them). She knows that these women will never threaten her, nor even question her.

Patty doesn't feel comfortable around the strong women

who have the creative ideas and who don't do the work Patty's way. Even if you've been doing an outstanding job and are in line for a promotion, Patty will tell her boss that your coworker Penny Placid deserves the raise instead because she's been there so long and has earned the opportunity (and because Penny never causes any trouble).

Personally, I've always preferred to reward the women who could do the job better than I. You don't get to the top by making safe promotions. People who are smarter than you and who have more potential will ultimately make you look better, because you are all on the same team. The boss usually doesn't know which particular person is responsible for what; he or she just cares that the group performed well.

The final woman to watch out for is *Ursula Unreliable*. Ursula is younger than Queen Bea, and much sharper. She portrays herself as a great friend of women, and she usually is—but only up to a certain point. Deep inside Ursula's psyche is her belief that her fundamental validity derives from the praise of men, not women.

Ursula Unreliable wants to be an active player on the women's team, but she's the product of the society around her, which has taught her that women are not as important as men, and that power and leadership are male attributes.

As Ursula was rising, women were her friends and supporters and she saw herself as part of the women's team. But when she got closer to the top, she saw fewer female role models and decided that the power players to whom she must be loyal are men. In general, she hasn't been able to integrate her desire to achieve with her earlier commitment to other women. She speaks up for women when it's easy, but her dedication collapses when the situation gets sticky. She's not willing to risk any of her hard-earned capital for other women. Because she wants to look good and get ahead, she will always desert the women and side with the guys.

Ursula is particularly dangerous because she looks like your friend. And she is, until the chips are down. The best way to deal with Ursula: Never take it for granted that she's on your side. She's not a bad person, but if you think that once she gets the Big Job she's going to remember you, or any other woman, you will be sorely disappointed.

• • •

Keep in mind when dealing with all these women: A strong team is always made up of different sorts of players with different expertise. So while you may think that Sue or Olivia is a pain, the boss probably has a reason to keep these women around. They fit as players on his or her team. Avoid their bad sides whenever possible and learn whatever you can from them. Never get into the position where you feel you must knock these women off.

There's still another reason why all these women have a tougher time at the office. When it comes to leaving the company, men tend to leave in teams. They attach themselves to a rising star and they rise together. When the star leaves, they leave together. The business section is always filled with stories of guys leaving with guys. How often do you hear about women leaving in droves with other women? I can't think of a single example.

The woman stays. And then she has to prove herself with the new bosses. She can't relax and fit into the team because she is always trying to impress—yet again—the new set of male players. She may be short of time and temper, but that's partly because her game is twice as hard to play as the guys'. So another way to deal with the Irenes and Ursulas is to try to understand how they got to be that way, and if you can help them, you will be doing a favor not just for them, and you, but for the entire team.

Some day, when the women's team solidifies, women will move in successful groups as the men do. Or they may actively choose to stay put because that's the right move for them. But whichever decision they make, they won't be left out.

11

The Eleven Most Common
Team Questions
(and Answers)

Not long ago I had to give three speeches in three days to three different women's organizations. The talks all seemed to go well, and I tried to vary the subject—not because anyone in the audience would have heard the other speeches, but because I find it boring to say the same thing over and over again.

Yet, regardless of my topic, I heard the audience ask the same handful of questions. I made a note of them, and realized in my next speeches that the same questions came up again. These questions range all over the map, from sports to politics. Here they are, with the answers. (And, yes, these are all real questions.)

Do I have to play golf?

I'm startled at how often this question comes up—perhaps more than any other. It even arises as a double-check on advice the questioners have received from other female lecturers who have told them that, indeed, they should play.

My answer is a ringing "no." You won't succeed at anything in business if it doesn't feel authentic. If you're not comfortable playing golf, it won't help you.

Nor will it get you anywhere if you try too hard. One audience member, a private banker, told me that she learned golf when it seemed as though her entire company was playing it. Eventually she realized she was attacking the game exactly the same way she attacked difficult problems at the office. She was taking private lessons, furiously hitting balls at the driving range, obsessively practicing on putting greens—she was trying to become Elizabeth Expert-at-Golf. And she was doing it all alone.

"I turned golf into a solitary sport because I wasn't ready to expose myself to anyone," she said. She knew many of the guys were no better at it than she was, yet they were charging off to the greens every weekend. "Why aren't they embarrassed?" she asked.

That's because golf is seldom about the actual game. Much of it is the camaraderie. And in that spirit, you have to feel comfortable making a fool of yourself when you make a bad shot.

Yes, occasionally a young man who's a terrific golfer will enter the company, and within months the boss will ask him to shoot a round, and people will say that this proves the power of golf. But these are rare occurrences. Few people are great golfers.

So, if you want to take up golf, know that it can help, but only if you really like it and can relax into it. There is no advantage to playing if it just becomes another form of work.

Find another way to build normal, relaxed relationships with your workmates and clients. I know many women who give small dinner parties or who organize weekend get-togethers. One friend told me that because she genuinely loves football, she gets tickets for her staff and takes them to the games. Another woman said that she and a friend started a bowling league for the nongolfers. Any activity that you genuinely enjoy, and that allows you to relax with higher-ups outside the office, can take the place of that game of golf.

(By the way, the men always close the deal in the locker room anyway, and you'll never get there, no matter how good a golfer you are.)

Will the men become unhappy if they think the women are banding together?

This question, asked in different formats, is probably the second-most common one I hear. The simple answer: This is not about the men. Nor is this about our relationship with men. This is about our relationship with other women.

I'm not saying anything negative about men. I love men. Most of my best bosses were men (actually, almost all my bosses, good or bad, were men). But I'm not writing a book to inspire them. I want to help women. Anyway, my experience has taught me that much of what the women want to change isn't all that different from what many of the men would change if given a chance.

So this isn't about the guys. But don't throw it in their faces. You are not playing on the women's team to the exclusion of playing on the Big Team. All we are saying is that there is a subteam called the women's team, and, like it or not, you're already on it, so use it to your best advantage.

That said, it's not a great idea to tell the guys that all the senior women have become mentors to the junior women to help them get promoted, and that the poor guys will have to figure it out on their own. That kind of discussion doesn't help anyone.

And if the men still feel threatened? That's their problem. See it as an opportunity for you to learn how to deal with threatened coworkers. As you achieve more and rise on the ladder, many people will be threatened—men as well as women. It's just part of the game. You might as well learn to accept and play it.

My boss is a woman, but she seems to demand more from me than she does from the men. Is there anything I can do about it?

This is one of the toughest questions asked. My sense is that many women who become bosses actually do expect more of the females on their staffs than the males. That boss has worked hard to get where she is, and has made many sacrifices. Now here you come, another woman, and she wants you to shine too. Part of the way she expresses her hope is to hold you to a higher level of expectation. She wants you to be better. She may expect you to make sacrifices, too.

Unfortunately, she may not see how hard she's driving you. Hostility builds. You think you are being treated unfairly; she doesn't understand why you aren't doing a better job than everyone else. Neither of you talk it over.

And that's the best way to sort this out: Talk to her. Get it all out in the open. (Caution: Make sure that you go directly to your boss when something is bothering you rather than discussing it with everyone else. She'll find out soon enough, making matters worse. It will also get back to her if you try going over her head. Then you create an even more unpleasant situation.)

When you talk to her, make it a nonblame conversation. Don't discuss women or gender. Sit down with her and say, "I feel as though I am not doing the job quite the way you expect it." Or, "You seem to have different expectations of me than of the others. I would appreciate some time to talk about it."

Be specific about the areas where you feel she has made it harder for you. Help her out. If you are vague, she may never understand your complaint.

If you tell her that she is treating you differently because you are a woman, you will put her on the defensive. Anyway, you don't know what kind of feelings she really has; you're tapping into a territory that's hard to understand. She probably doesn't understand it herself. Few of us do. Maybe she does have faith in you and is just pushing you harder than others. Maybe she's one of the women we talked about in the last chapter, and her issues result from her need to be perfect, or from her fear of failure.

Keep in mind: If the problem doesn't get fixed in a reasonable amount of time, you may need to consider leaving. If she can't understand your issues, and a private straightforward conversation gets you nowhere, you're probably in a dead end.

Also consider this: Is it possible that *you* are treating your boss differently because she's female? One woman told me she had a secretary named Gina who made coffee for every man she ever worked for. But when Gina became her secretary, she stopped doing it. It turned out that Gina, who was an excellent secretary in every other way, resented making coffee for another woman, plain and simple.

Perhaps, like Gina, you have some gender issues of your own concerning your female boss, possibly ones you're not even aware of. Could that be the reason she is treating you differently?

I've just been promoted and some of the men are challenging my authority. How do I get them to respect me?

Guys always challenge authority. They will challenge you, too. Just don't get caught in these tests. If you move through the first assault well, they will soon end.

Here's a specific question I received from a woman in the audience at one of my recent lectures: She'd just started at her new position and had a dozen men reporting to her. The first time something went wrong, one of the men went over her head to her boss, who then approached her and said, "I guess you're having problems with Jim. He's concerned about your skills. What can I do to help?"

"How should I have handled the situation?" the woman asked.

I told her she should have told her boss something like this: "I'm new in the job and these kind of things happen. I will come to you if I have problems or if I need something. But please let me deal with Jim. He now reports to me."

In other words, build confidence with your boss that you can deal with the issue. Then approach Jim and say, "This isn't how it works here. We all make mistakes. If anyone needs to know about our errors, I will tell them. But we're a team, and you are on my team, and we all play together. If you have a complaint or a problem, come to me."

You must do this in a way that doesn't make you sound like his mother, his schoolteacher, or a nun. Do it in a way that leaves everyone's dignity intact.

So, know that you will be challenged, and when you are, don't attack the challenger. Just let him know you are aware of what's going on, and it will be okay. Too often when women get in this position, they wilt, feeling they can't win. Or, they turn into a viper and go for the jugular.

Keep your cool—and your sense of proportion. Is your job at risk? Or are you facing a small annoyance? Don't respond to every challenge the same way.

Another tactic: Try as hard as possible not to let the male stereotype of women throw you. For example, the men may expect that you'll be overwhelmed by your new responsibilities. And it's true that your life balance is different from theirs. Maybe you have two kids at home, or a sick mother you're tending. But you must present the image of the confident businessperson who knows how to get the job done, no matter what. You might even be able to avoid challenges if you look as though you'll coast right through them.

Keep in mind: People like to be attached to power. They like to work with people who are comers. By and large men don't think women are as powerful as men, in part because they aren't, pecking order–wise. Thus you must build your male staff's confidence that you are as concerned about their careers as any male boss would be, and that as you ascend the totem pole, the men who helped you along the way will ascend with you. That's part of the power game.

As mentioned, when a top man leaves the company to take a new job, his guys usually end up going with him. When a woman moves ahead, she's not well known for taking her people with her. She arrives at her new position and tries to figure out how to give all the people there a fair chance.

The guys may give the old staff the same chance, too, but they're more likely to want their own team in place. So having a female boss can look less powerful because the chances of profiting from it in the long run seem less likely.

To remedy this, make them know they are part of your team. You are motivating them because you want everyone to move ahead together. It's not just about your career. It's about everyone's career.

The men tell me I am too aggressive. What should I do?

You can't be afraid of being aggressive.

If you are aggressive in the most positive sense of the word, you may simply be doing such an excellent job that the others around you feel threatened. Maybe they had things their way for a long time, and now you've come in and upset their applecart.

Still, don't be so aggressive that you steamroller your coworkers. If you're going to be a dynamo, do it with a sense of camaraderie, lightness, and humor. Don't make the word *aggressive* synonymous with *bitch*. Make it synonymous with *excellence*.

At the same time, take care not to land in the trap I see so many aggressive women fall into—toning themselves down because they fear that being too successful will make the men think they are offensive.

Remember the story from the first chapter about the ambitious young woman whose male colleagues told her that she was generating too much revenue? She couldn't step out of her own skin enough to understand that she was setting a new standard in the department. The guys were trying to scare her off a little. It almost worked.

Are you playing on the team and turning into the top performer? Or are you a loner who's out to beat everyone and anyone else? Try to figure out whether the men are using the word *aggressive* to keep you from demanding too much of them, or to stop you from being genuinely unpleasant.

These days no one gets away with being brutal. The people

on top are as human as the ones just starting out; they just have a more complex job. I firmly believe that, in business, good people will eventually win.

As I become more successful, should I stop sitting with the women at the meetings and instead sit with the men?

Another way to put this question: Is where you sit a meaningful issue? Do you try to be one of the guys, or do you show your solidarity by surrounding yourself with your female colleagues? If you think this matter has nothing to do with you, you're probably in denial.

Most of us are more at ease when we're with other women. That's human nature: We're all more comfortable spending time with people who are like us than people who aren't. There's not much you can do about that.

My answer: You probably shouldn't sit only with the women now, but at the same time you don't want the women to think you're not one of them anymore. So find another woman to sit next to you at important meetings. Make a statement for both of you. Show that you're comfortable being with the men, but you haven't forgotten you are still on the women's team.

The principle that there is safety in numbers applies throughout the work world. As women obtain more power, we will discover that the more of us there are, the more comfortable we will feel. For example, if you're the only woman in the office who's pregnant, your paranoia may not be out of line. But if several other women are also pregnant, you'll feel less vulnerable.

Whenever you can enlist another woman to help you break through on the uncomfortable issues, you'll feel better. All the more reason to join the team.

How can I take the time to be part of the team? I'm so busy already.

First and foremost, you are already part of the team.

That said, my expectation for all women is that, as we start being smarter about our work, we will have more free time at our disposal.

Too many of us are trapped in the total-time-at-the-job myth: We think we are showing our dedication when we come in an hour earlier and leave two hours later than everyone else. The reality is that people wonder why it takes us three more hours to get our work done than anyone else. Those old adages from our grandparents' generation, including the one that says keep your nose close to the grindstone and someone will notice you, are not smart business strategies for today.

The more you focus on getting your job done in a fast and efficient manner, the more time you will have to do the other necessary parts of the job, such as networking and mentoring. Having lunch with a senior colleague will do more to advance your career than another hour spent toiling at the office.

Another myth women still swallow is that we have to do everything just right. Remember Polly Perfect? We'll spend ten agonizing hours, or all weekend, making sure that our presentation is flawless. We lose sight of the fact that lining a few important people up on our side before a meeting, and doing the other appropriate politicking through our network, is probably more important in getting the proposal approved than all those extra hours of working on the actual presentation.

When we let go of some of these perfection issues, we will see that we don't need to find extra time to play on the team. We need to use the time we have more efficiently. Indeed, by being part of the team, you will actually save time. Instead of having to do everything yourself, you will have people to call for advice and help. Instead of having to speak up for yourself at every meeting, you will have created built-in support. Instead of not knowing that a great new job is opening up in another part of the company, you will have advance information—and you'll be ready to use your contacts to apply for it.

The best part of being on the team: It's easier to manage your time because you have help doing it.

How do I toot my own horn and still be a team player?

Women tend to interpret the rules too literally. After my last book was published, women asked me question after question regarding how to follow all the rules of business, even though the book specifically says that you need to follow only those rules that make the most sense for you. Just as men refuse to look at a map when they get lost, women tend to regard the map, or any other guide, as an absolute truth that will take them wherever they want to go.

The women who ask the above question think tooting your own horn means one and only one thing: bragging to everyone about what a good little worker you are. How obnoxious that sounds.

What we don't give enough thought to: Tooting can mean many things, and apply to many situations differently. For example, if you are a successful team leader, you don't want to brag about yourself. Instead, you tell everyone what a great job your team did—in other words, you bask in the reflected glory rather than the limelight.

Here's a great related strategy: Whenever one of my employees performed well, I always sent a note to a higher boss asking him to get in touch with my staffer and compliment her on a fabulous job. Invariably, a few hours later I would hear from my excited employee telling me about the Big Boss's praise. The boss would thank me, too, for connecting him to the employee.

Well, I've just tooted my own horn as well. The boss knows my team has excelled, and both he and the woman under me see that I give credit where credit is due. That's being a smart team member. Everyone wins.

Just as a team is only as strong as its weakest link, it is made more powerful by its strongest link. If you are out there getting it known, you are helping everyone. There's no disconnect between being a team player and being a star.

So toot your own horn any reasonable way possible. If

the company newsletter wants to write about you, don't be demure and hide. Smarten up. You are making the team more important because now it has a player in the news.

Every time you go to a meeting outside your office, every time you work with a new client, every time you appear in public, your actions reflect on your entire team. Some women have twisted the notion of playing on a team into giving up their identity. It doesn't mean that. It means individual excellence, accomplished together.

Do I really have to play the game? I don't want to.

Whenever I hear this one, I get flip. "Then why are you here?" I ask.

Business is a game. You are already on a team. That's it.

Yes, if you don't want to play, you can sit in your office and do your work and expect little in return. I'm not saying that's a bad choice. You probably won't get anywhere, but you'll be left alone and if that's what you want, fine. I know many good women who have chosen that path.

If this is your call, however, don't whine about not getting ahead, and the discrimination you face, and how little money you're making. You can't have it both ways. Either you play or you don't.

Frankly, I think that some of the women who say they don't want to compete have a problem: a holier-than-thou attitude that says they're better people because they don't like playing games. These women say this because they assume the game, and most of its serious players, are bad.

I suspect this attitude also can be a defense mechanism for those who are afraid to get in there and try harder. It allows those women to hold on to the old ways of doing things and pretend those are the only ways.

Also: Many times I have a heard a woman who wasn't doing well explain it away by saying: "I just won't play the game. I'm above that."

No one's told you that you absolutely must play. As mentioned, plenty of women (and men) don't want to. But if you're interested in succeeding, playing the game will help you achieve your goals. Pretending that you're not playing in order to cover your failures isn't going to impress anyone.

Remember: Don't play if you don't want to. But then, don't expect to win, either.

Can I have both a family and a career?

Yes, you can. You are the architect of your own life. You decide what you want and how to get it.

But can you have it all at once? Probably not. I don't think anyone can rev all her engines at full speed, twenty-four hours a day. And there's seldom a reason anyone should have to.

Once upon a time we started working for a company when we were young, and we expected to retire from it when we were old. Today is a new world. Over the course of a career we'll work for several different companies, and maybe even have several careers.

If your plans involve marriage and children, you may decide to lower the heat on your work life and up the heat on your family life for a while. You can always jump-start your career when you're ready. (This is one of the prime reasons to maintain your web, even when you're not working. This way, when you're ready to return, you don't have to worry about starting from scratch—you've already got all your ducks in a row.)

Contrary to popular myth, work is not an express train leaving the station so fast that if you decide to get off and have kids, you can never reboard. You can indeed. I did. After raising my three kids, I went back to work and advanced much farther than I had before I'd left. I know countless other women whose successful careers were interrupted by time off for family. The distinguished jurist (now retired) Judge Patricia Wald, of the U.S. Court of Appeals for the D.C. Circuit, took ten years off in the middle of her legal career to raise five children. She later returned to work and eventually was appointed by President Carter to the circuit court.

It's the difference between simultaneous and sequential. In other words, you can have it all, but you can't have it all at once. You can work for a while, slow down when your family is young, and then go back to work full speed at the same, or a different job.

When more women are working together on the team, we will finally achieve what we need to make work and family life balanced. Today those few companies where job sharing and excellent maternity benefits are in place are the companies where women are leading the charge, making sure that the workplace is supportive of anyone who wants a family.

One of the greatest benefits of playing on the team is achieving a critical mass of women in important positions who understand the issues. Today, many of those in positions of power are men who have wives at home who've never worked, or who have nannies and caretakers; or they are women who never made the decision to marry or have families.

As the team becomes more female-inclusive, it will have a more varied group of women with more diverse opinions making the big decisions.

Note: Balancing work and family can be much harder for entrepreneurs. You have more freedom to create your own hours, but on the flip side, if your business demands you be there, be there you must. You don't have as much support as you would at a larger outfit.

Many small companies have only a few employees at best, and something like an illness can create a real crisis. This makes it even more necessary to have a solid team behind you. Recently a friend who ran a small retail business came down with a serious ailment and was hospitalized for a month, so three of her best friends stepped in and ran her shop. They may not have done as good a job as my friend, but they were able to give her exactly the help she needed.

My office feels split, but it's not about the men and the women. It's a problem between the older and the younger women. Why can't we all just get along?

This question, which surprised me when I first heard it, comes up more often than not.

The older women in the workplace frequently feel that if not for them, the younger women wouldn't have the same opportunities. These older women want to feel appreciated. They were often trailblazers, the first ones to achieve this rank or reach that plateau. They have suffered everything from gender discrimination to sexual harassment.

They also feel the younger women, who don't understand that there's still a sex-based battle going on, act frivolously. And, they can be jealous of the younger women's education, which puts them on a more equal level with the men. They think these younger women want it all—the job, the marriage, the family—whereas many of the older women feel they had to sacrifice one if not all of these goals to reach their current position.

And, of course, many of these women were willing to take low-paying entry-level jobs in order to get on the executive track. They feel the younger women refuse to pay their dues the way most of the older women did.

Meanwhile, the younger women think the older women are too old-fashioned, too serious, and their ideas are too rigid; everything they say reeks of, "This is how it must be done," and "This is how things are." The older women seem angry, unhappy, and willing to be no more than alter egos for the men.

The younger women also find the older women—who often entered the work force thinking they would stay at the same company their entire life—stuck. The older women tend to preach homilies to the younger women when they threaten to leave if they don't get what they want. The older women expect the younger ones to display company loyalty, and they find its absence immature and selfish.

There is nothing to be gained from these intergenerational spats. Both groups of women have a contribution to make—especially if they stop thinking of themselves as younger and older and instead think of themselves as teammates. A team operates for the benefit of all. It's not about who is right and who is wrong. Both groups are right for their time and place.

Women must learn to respect and understand each other. The younger ones have to understand that the older ones did indeed blaze a trail, making it possible for others of the same sex to have a successful career. They stood up when it was dangerous to do so, even if today it doesn't look that way.

Meanwhile, the older women have to learn to live by their words. If they are truly trying to create female/male parity, they mustn't become upset when the young women seem to act more like the guys than the girls.

By sharing their knowledge of the pitfalls and roadblocks, the older women can streamline the learning curve for the younger women. Institutional knowledge of departments, as well as practices and personalities, is invaluable for an ambitious young woman. But the older women have to know that their younger friends will take this information and apply it to the game their own way.

Younger women can help the older women, too. They can teach them that this job isn't the only game in town, and that suffering in silence isn't always necessary. Further, their nontraditional thinking and behavior can often add some joy and welcome relief to the workplace. In many ways I think of myself as the old fogy around the office, and I know the younger women brighten up my day even when they act out of the box. No matter—their attitude is usually refreshing and stimulating.

The younger women will make it in ways we older women never imagined. Yes, we paved the path for them. Now we need to join with them and celebrate what we have created.

Conclusion

One argument that women often hear as to why we're not in the top echelons of business: We haven't been in the pipeline long enough. By the next generation, the men tell us, things will be different. So, the reasoning might go, why should we work as a team when in just a few years we'll achieve parity?

Will we really? Remember that Catalyst report on the legal profession, which stated that only 12 percent of all partners are women—and a similar percentage applies to the number of chief counsels in corporate America. Here's a profession where women have been well represented for well over a generation, where the playing field is as level as it can be (unlike the usual corporate structure), where there are more women than men in law schools. Yet women are as stymied in law as they are everywhere else.

In fact, I give more speeches to female lawyers than to women in any other profession. They know that things aren't right and they are desperate to correct them. It's not about waiting for the next generation. It's about doing something now.

Here's more bad news from the prestigious Committee of 200, a twenty-year-old network of top women entrepreneurs and corporate leaders. The group recently completed its first-ever Business Leadership Index, showing how businesswomen fared in relation to men on a ten-point scale, with ten representing parity with men. In an aggregate of ten separate benchmarks, women scored an overall 3.95. Not very encouraging, especially considering that women are not really in the minority.

There are more of us than men in the general population, and we're getting closer to being the majority at work, too. We need to stop acting as if we are asking for a favor, for permission to exist. We need to start acting as if we have the right to be there. And we have to do this together.

For women, climbing the corporate ladder has more benefits than just better jobs, bigger salaries, and more power. We can create a much better world for our daughters and granddaughters in which to work and live. We can give them more options for their future by providing them with more career possibilities.

The fact is, it's good for business to have more women, for the same reason it's good to have more of any minority in business. All of us know best how to address our own needs; we seldom know how to address the needs of others. It follows that the products and services produced by a society will be better if the people making those products and services are the people who actually use them.

At the moment, this is not the case. While straight white men are still in the majority as business leaders, they no longer make up the majority of the population. As a result, many products and services aren't nearly as good, as user friendly, as they could be. American society is changing so quickly that if business doesn't begin adjusting to the reality of minorities—women, black, gay, and so on—the business landscape is going to be strewn with a lot of white elephants.

• • •

There is one message I want to highlight above all: Women are in this together—whether we want to be or not. So you might as well join with enthusiasm. Those of us who don't help each other, hurt each other. Everyone else sees you as part of this team. It's time you start seeing yourself that way.

Once you embrace the idea that you and the women around you are going to make it together and that you don't have to be a lone wolf, you will discover new ways to network and form teams.

Women have done everything else we've needed to do. We've armed ourselves with degrees. We've learned to play the men's game. We've challenged the status quo when necessary.

Now it's time to realize that if we want to go the final step, we must help each other.

This is our game to win or lose. Yet we keep tiptoeing around winning. We take a little step forward here, another step forward there, as long we feel the territory is safe. It reminds me of those old silent movies showing women bathing by the sea, slowly walking down to the water, gingerly dipping one toe into the ocean, withdrawing it, dipping again.

Most of the time these women never went in farther than their ankles. Likewise, too often we don't submerge ourselves today; we go no farther than where we have felt comfortable.

The past is past. It's time to move on. Business can't work without us. Think about it—the men can't kick us out now. It's too late.

But can they keep us subjugated? Not likely. We are too smart and too integral to making it work.

But we're not integral to being the most powerful part of the operating machine—not until some fundamental practices change. We have allowed ourselves to become the silent majority. It's time to end the silence. It's time to speak out. It's time to act.

My first book was one that men wanted women to read, because it helped women understand male behavior at the office, and that made the men's job easier.

This book is one that the men won't want women to read. They know that if women ever stop playing as isolated individuals and start playing as a team, all the rules are going to change. The men also know that when that happens, it's going to be a whole new ball game.

Acknowledgments

I want to thank all of the thousands of women whom I have had the opportunity to meet and talk to over the last two years. Spending a day, or even just a meal, at each of your companies and organizations has both humbled and inspired me. You have taught me that women all over the world just need a word of encouragement or a simple "Go for it!" to make huge strides in their careers as well as major changes in their lives. This book is for each of you, because it consists of all the remarkable lessons I have learned from your stories.

I'm also indebted to all the wonderful publishing professionals at Gotham Books, especially Lauren Marino, my excellent and supportive editor, and Bill Shinker, my wise and savvy publisher. Also, a resounding thank you to my energetic agent and friend Jan Miller, who helped me reinvent myself, as well as her great team of Michael, Shannon, and Carla.

Before closing, I have to send my love and kisses to all my gorgeous grandchildren: Drew, Sarah, Alec, Brian, and Eric. I promise you that your names will appear in every one of my books.

Finally, as always, I must mention my collaborator, Gene Stone, who brings me to life with the written word. Gene, you know how important you are to me and what a contribution you have made to my life. Thank you so very much for everything.